SOLO GUITAR   AUDIO ACCESS INCLUDED

VIDEO GAME MUSIC
FOR FINGERSTYLE GUITAR

T0088574

2   ANGRY BIRDS THEME

6   BABA YETU from CIVILIZATION IV

14   BOUNTY HUNTER
from ADVENT RISING

22   BRATJA (BROTHERS)
from FULL METAL ALCHEMIST

27   DEARLY BELOVED
from KINGDOM HEARTS

28   DON'T FORGET from DELTARUNE™

29   ELDER SCROLLS: OBLIVION

34   EYES ON ME
from FINAL FANTASY VIII

40   THEME FROM FALLOUT® 4

44   MAIN THEME
from FINAL FANTASY I

46   MAIN THEME
from FINAL FANTASY VII

50   MEGALOVANIA from UNDERTALE®

58   MINECRAFT: SWEDEN

57   SADNESS AND SORROW
from the television series NARUTO

60   THAT'S THE WAY IT IS
from RED DEAD REDEMPTION II

64   UNSHAKEN
from RED DEAD REDEMPTION II

72   Guitar Notation Legend

PLAYBACK+
Speed • Pitch • Balance • Loop

To access audio visit:
www.halleonard.com/mylibrary

Enter Code
2105-2722-4134-1134

ISBN 978-1-5400-5338-1

HAL•LEONARD®

For all works contained herein:
Unauthorized copying, arranging, adapting, recording, Internet posting, public performance,
or other distribution of the music in this publication is an infringement of copyright.
Infringers are liable under the law.

Visit Hal Leonard Online at
www.halleonard.com

Contact us:
Hal Leonard
7777 West Bluemound Road
Milwaukee, WI 53213
Email: info@halleonard.com

In Europe, contact:
Hal Leonard Europe Limited
42 Wigmore Street
Marylebone, London, W1U 2RN
Email: info@halleonardeurope.com

In Australia, contact:
Hal Leonard Australia Pty. Ltd.
4 Lentara Court
Cheltenham, Victoria, 3192 Australia
Email: info@halleonard.com.au

from ANGRY BIRDS

Angry Birds Theme

By Ari Pulkkinen

*Knock on body of gtr.
to create percussive sound.

Copyright © 2009 Rovio Entertainment Limited
This arrangement Copyright © 2020 Rovio Entertainment Limited
All Rights Administered Worldwide by Kobalt Songs Music Publishing
All Rights Reserved   Used by Permission

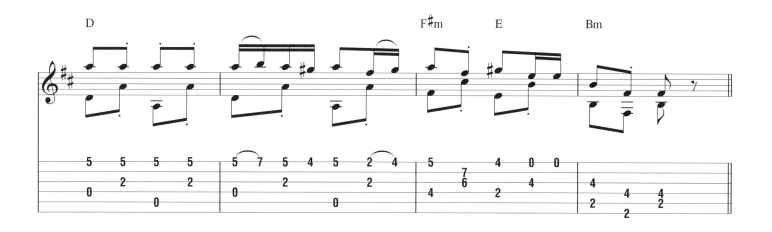

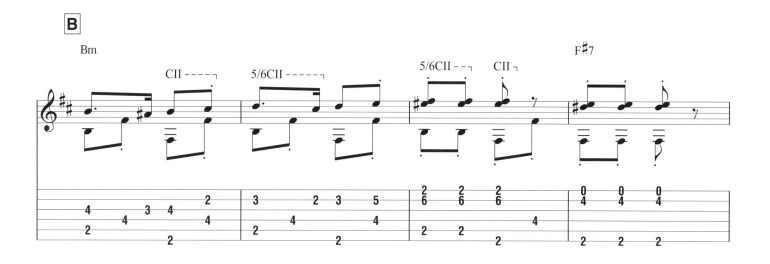

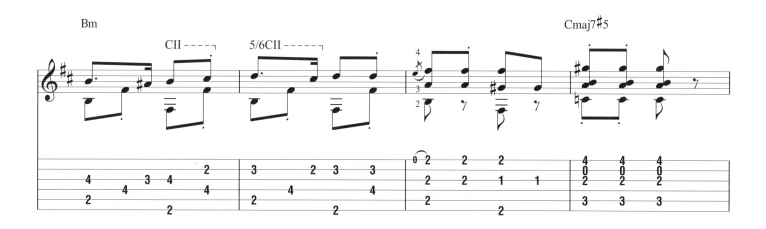

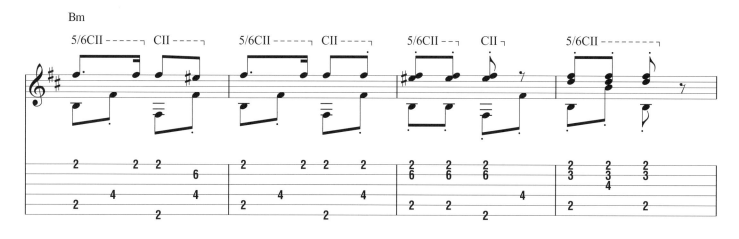

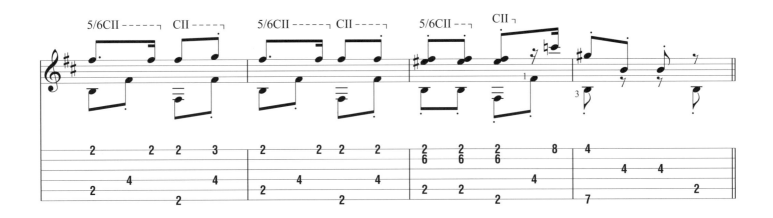

C

Bm

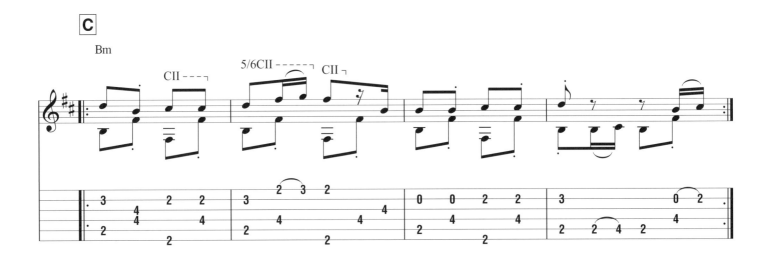

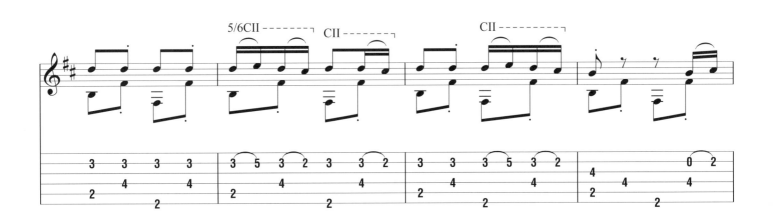

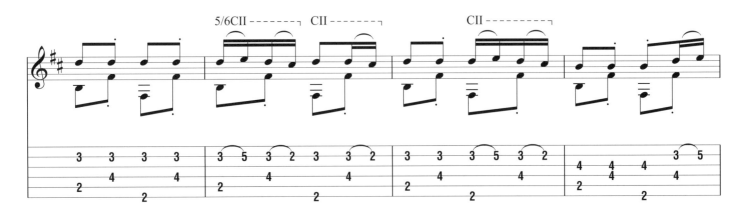

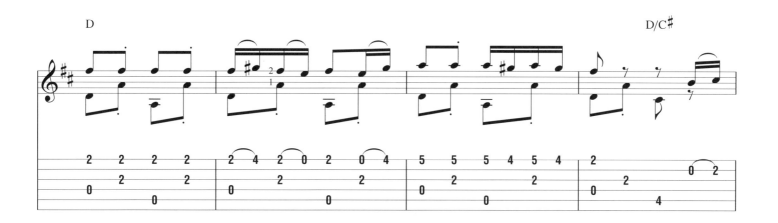

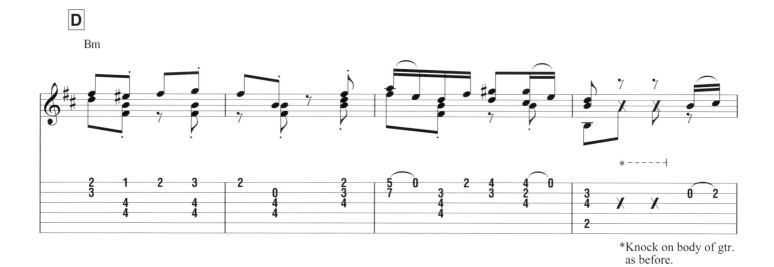

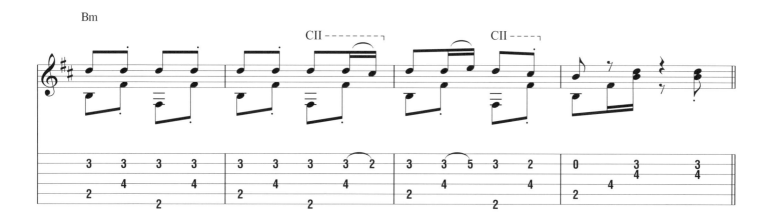

*Knock on body of gtr.
as before.

**As before.

Baba Yetu

Words and Music by Christopher Tin

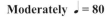

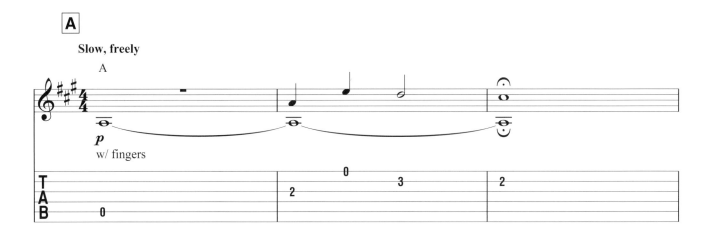

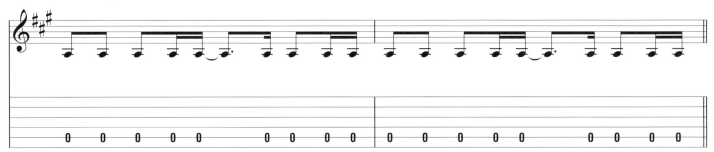

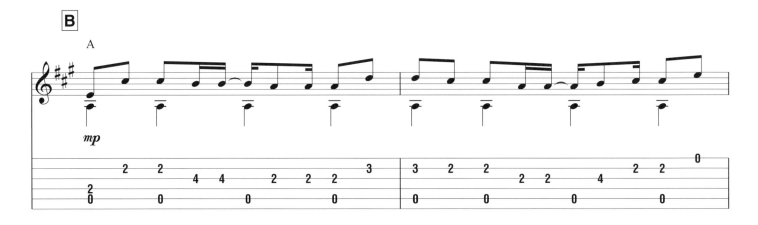

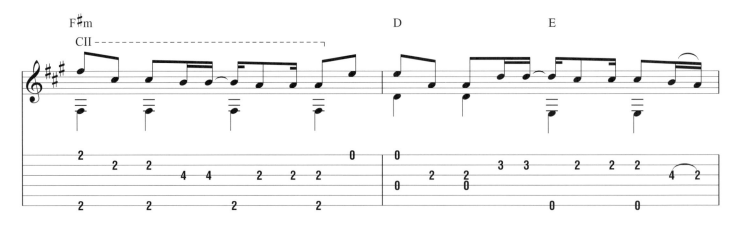

Copyright © 2005 2K Games Songs LLC
This arrangement Copyright © 2020 2K Games Songs LLC
All Rights Administered by Bike Music c/o Concord Music Publishing
All Rights Reserved   Used by Permission

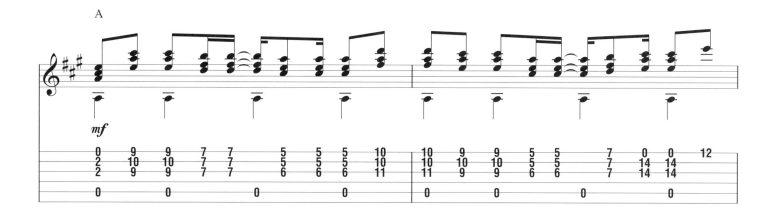

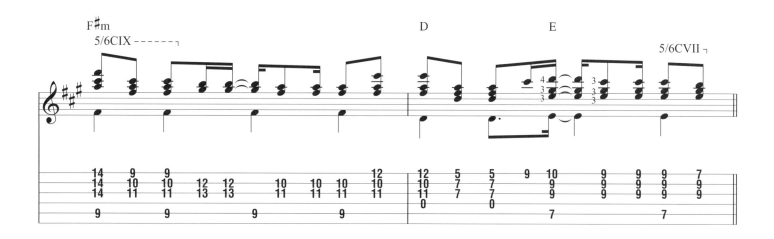

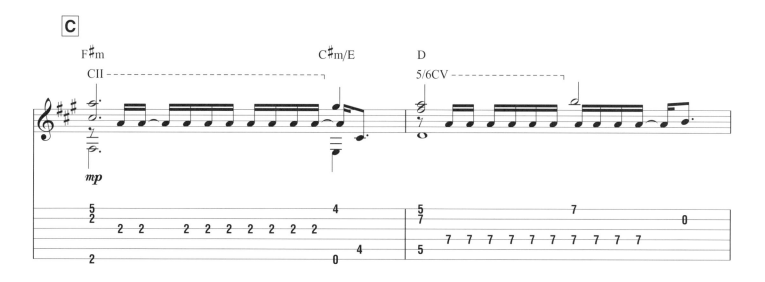

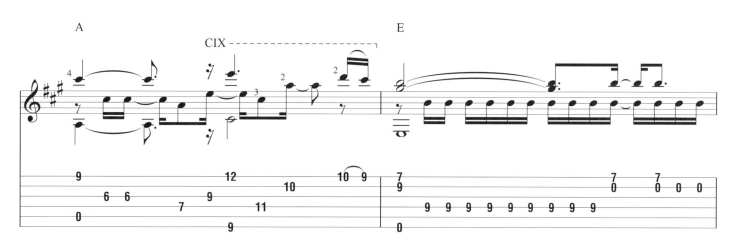

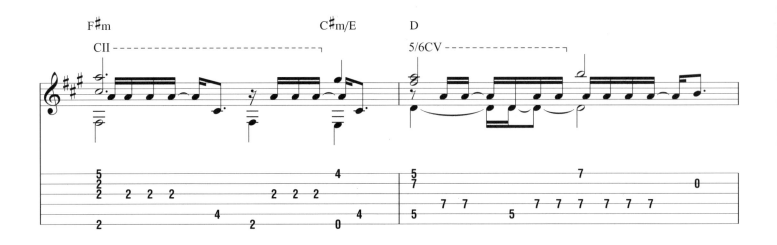

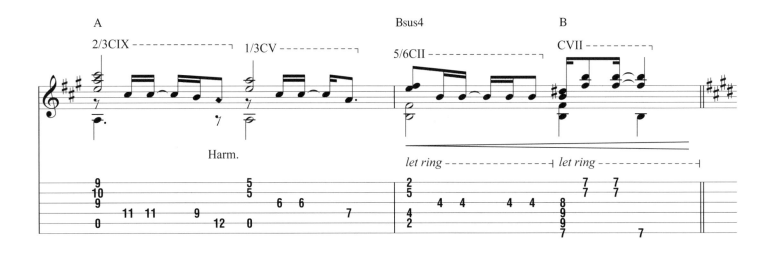

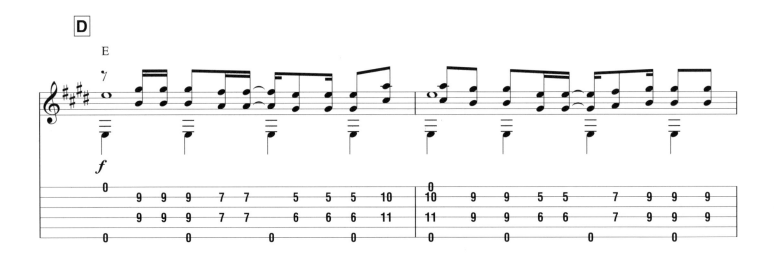

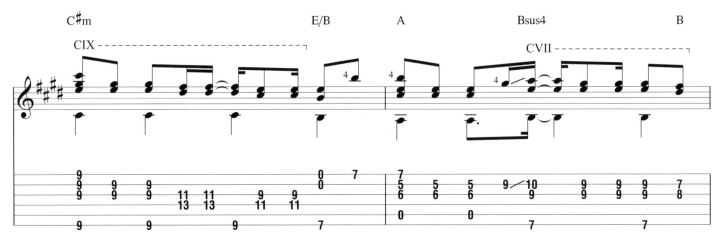

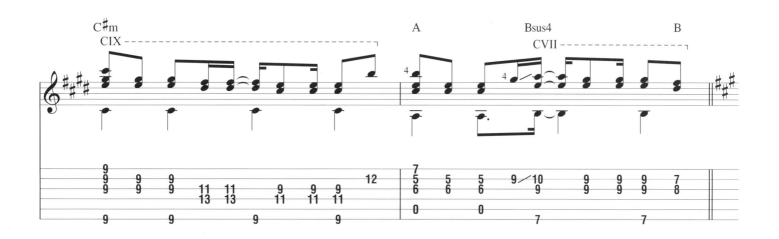

 E

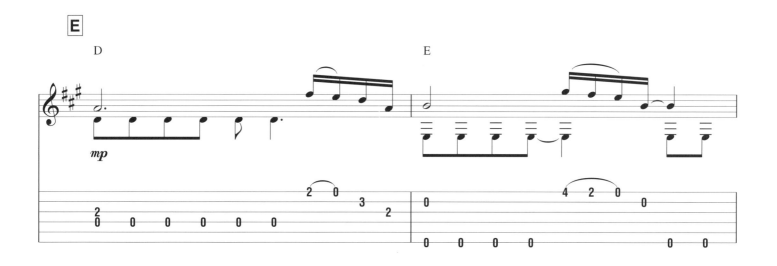

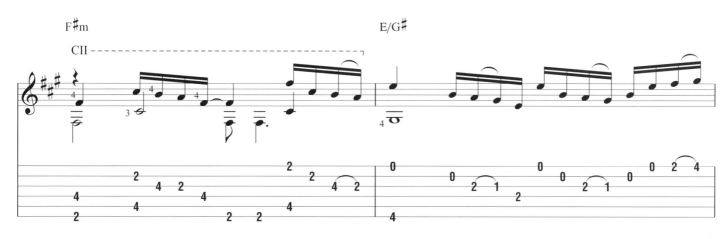

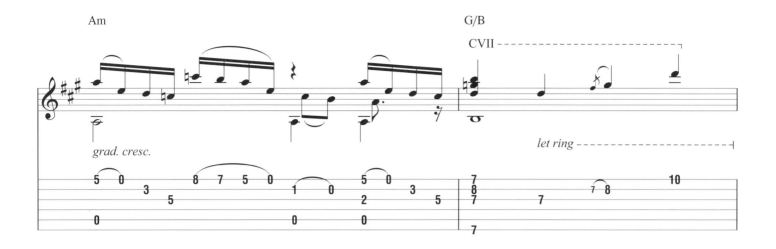

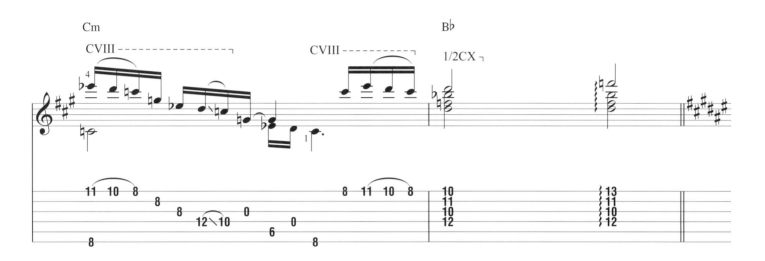

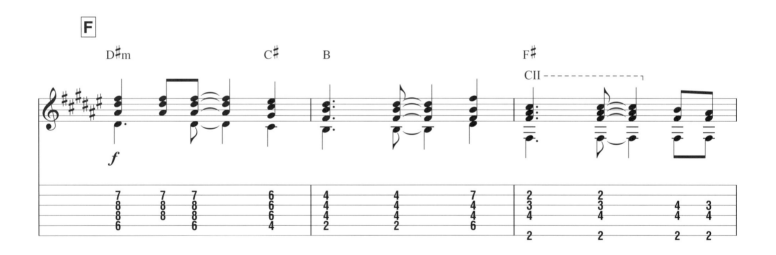

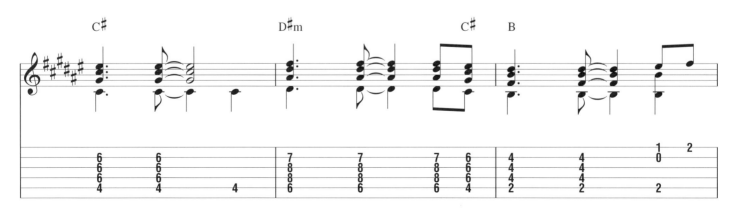

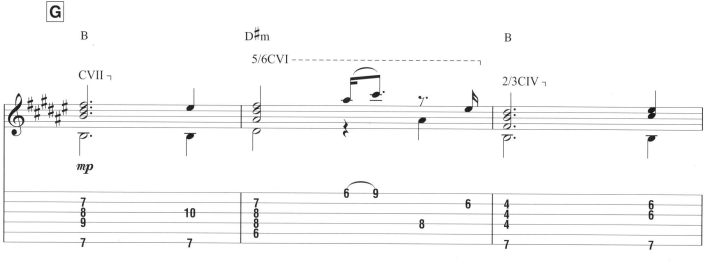

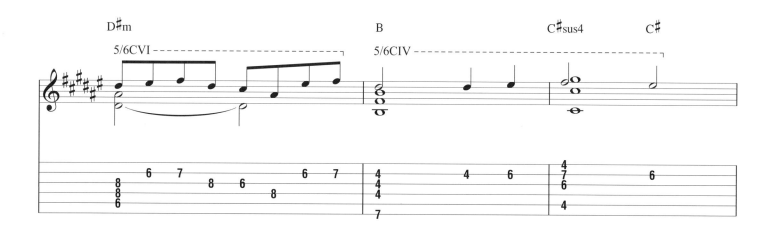

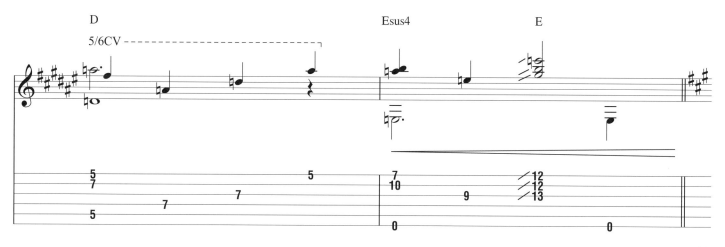

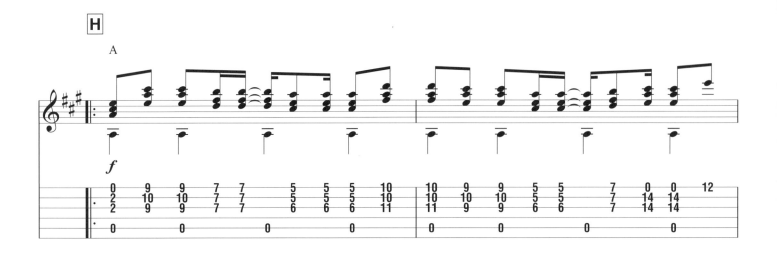

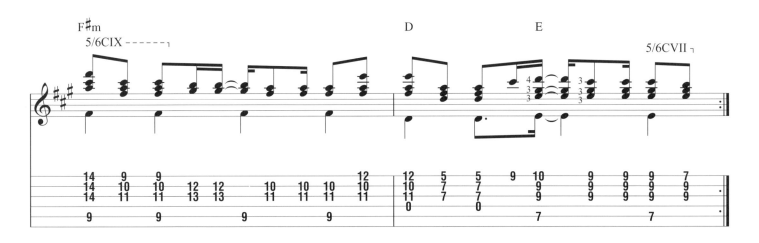

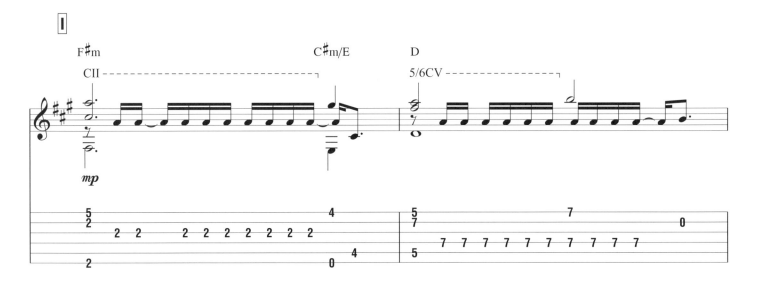

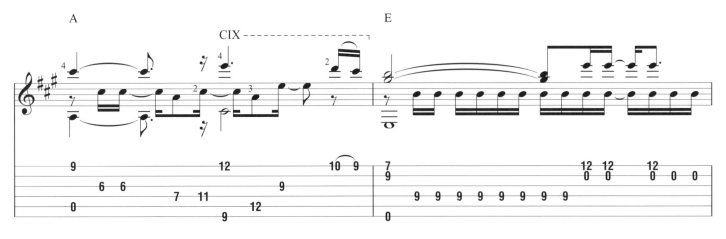

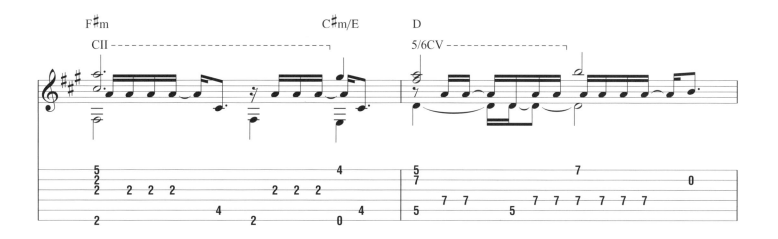

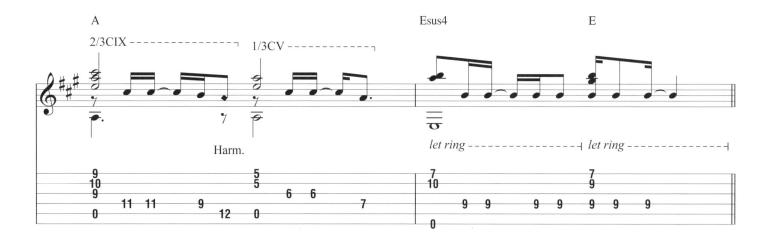

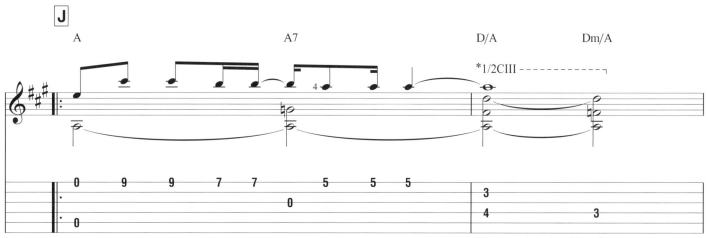

*Barre 2nd, 3rd & 4th strings.

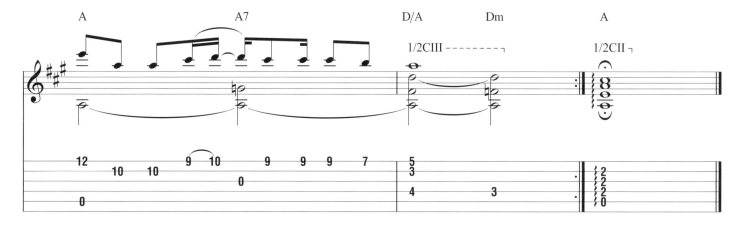

Bounty Hunter

By Tommy Tallarico

Tuning:
(low to high) D-A-D-G-A-D

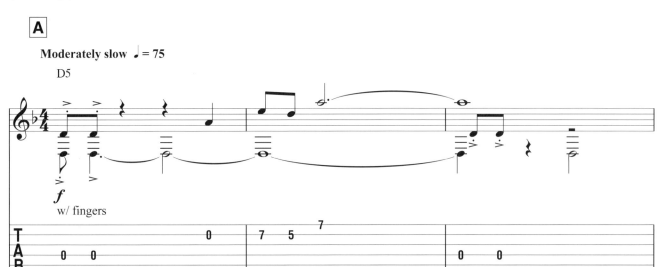

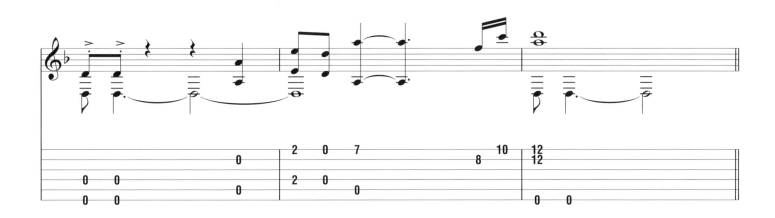

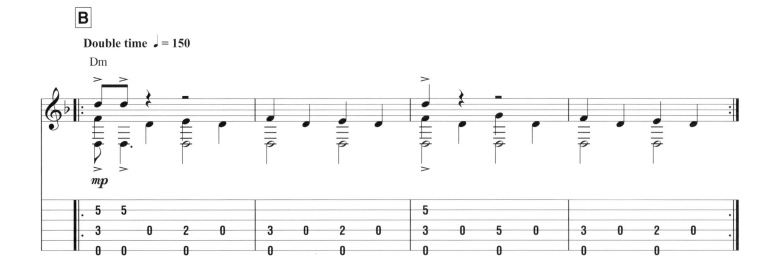

Copyright © 2007 Tallarico Music Publishing
This arrangement Copyright © 2020 Tallarico Music Publishing
All Rights Reserved   Used by Permission

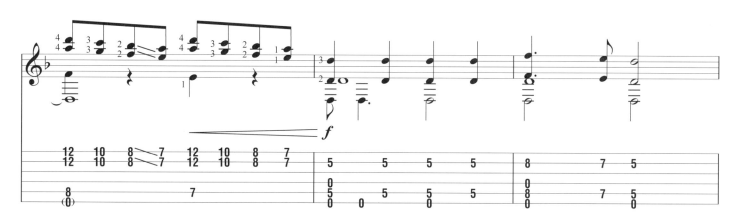

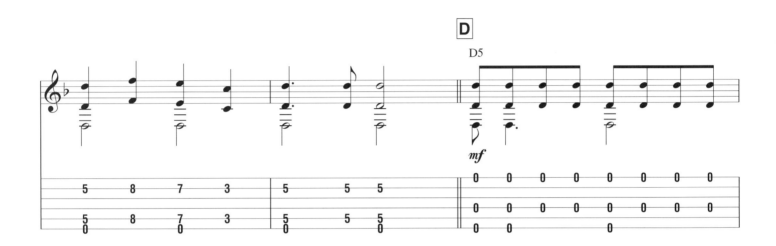

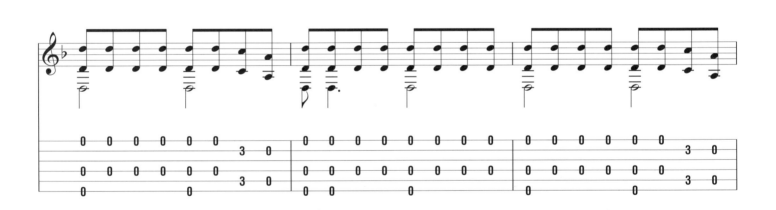

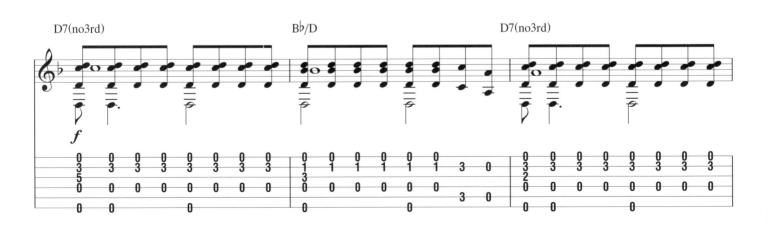

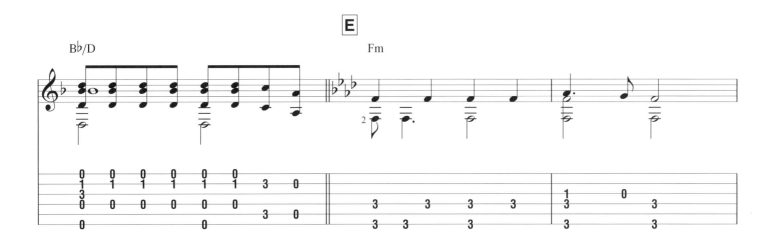

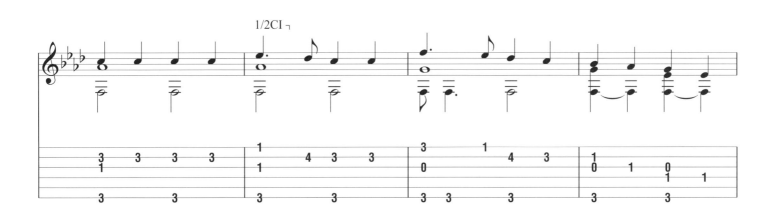

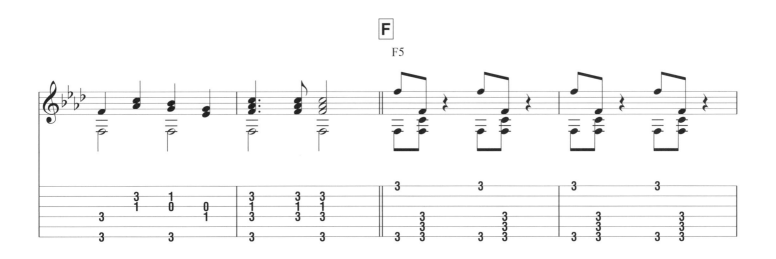

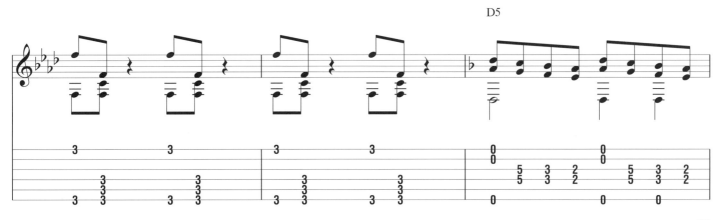

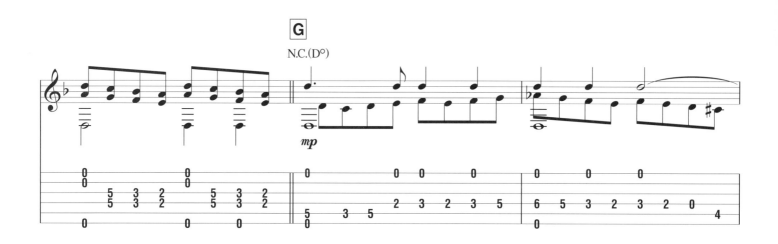

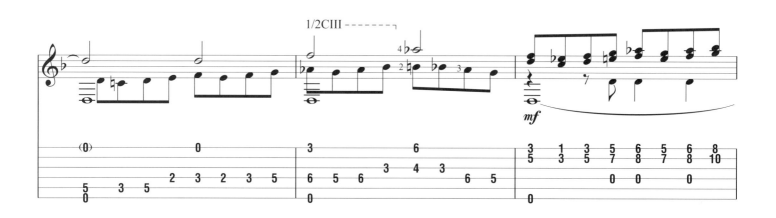

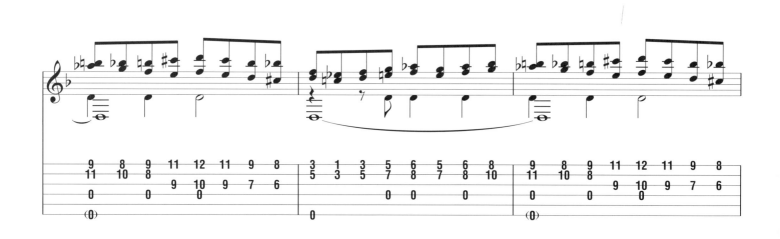

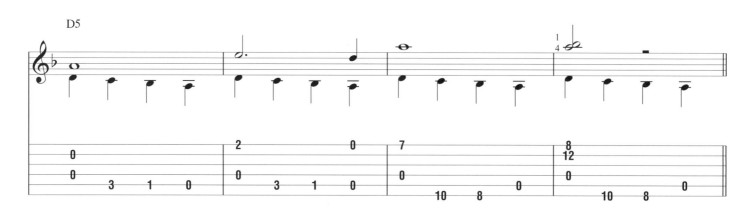

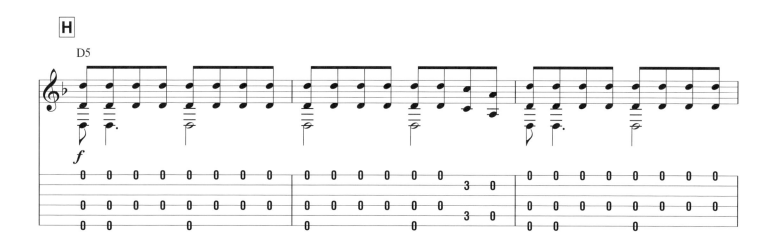

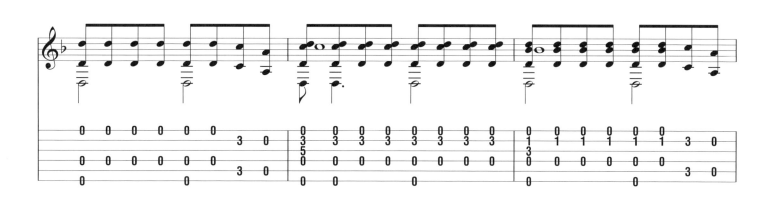

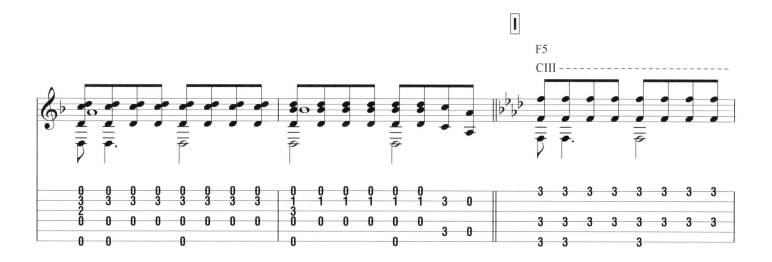

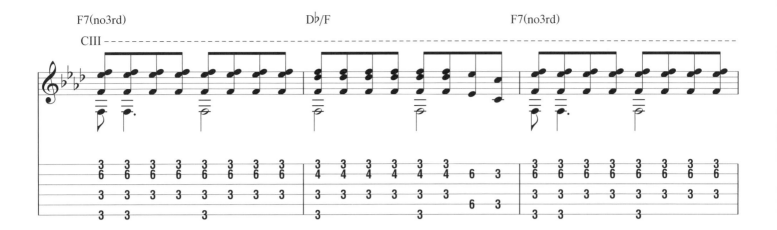

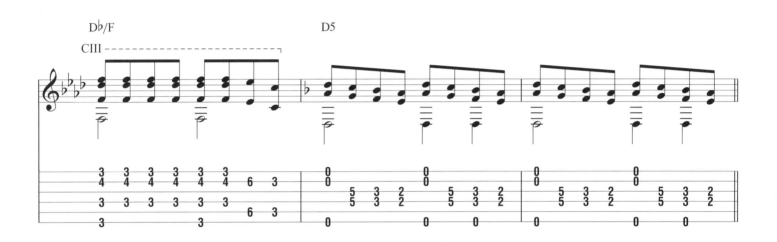

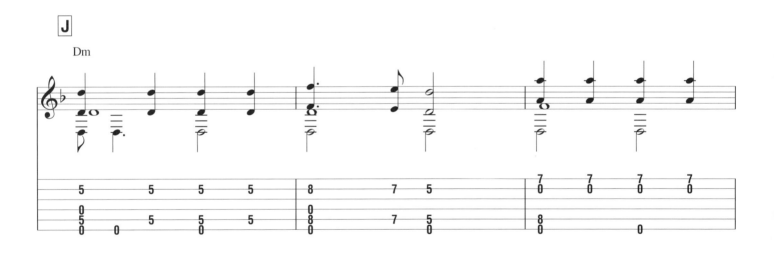

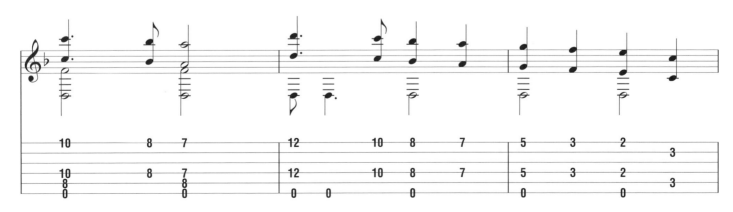

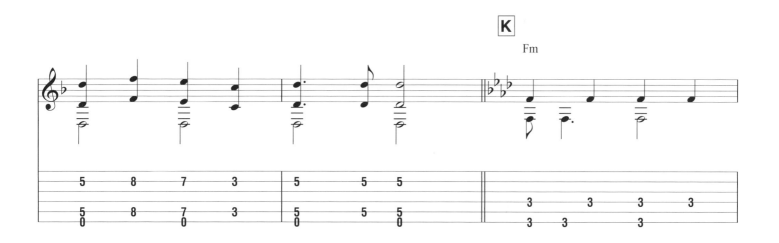

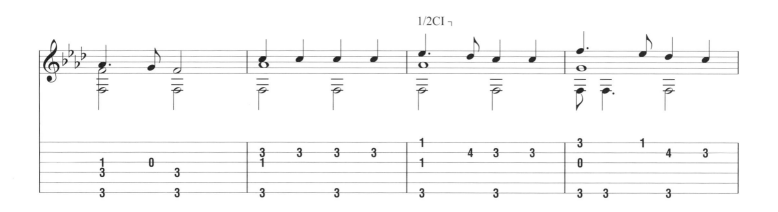

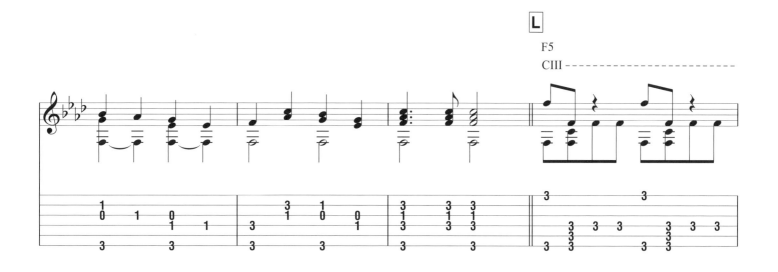

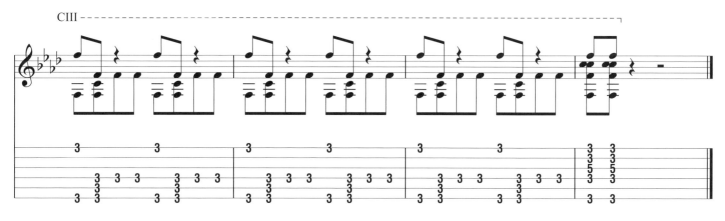

from **FULL METAL ALCHEMIST**

Bratja
(Brothers)

Capo V

Words and Music by Michiru Oshima, Seiji Mizushima and Tatiana Naumova

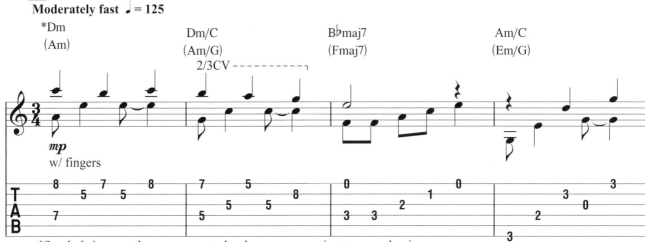

*Symbols in parentheses represent chord names respective to capoed guitar.
Symbols above reflect actual sounding chords. Capoed fret is "0" in tab.

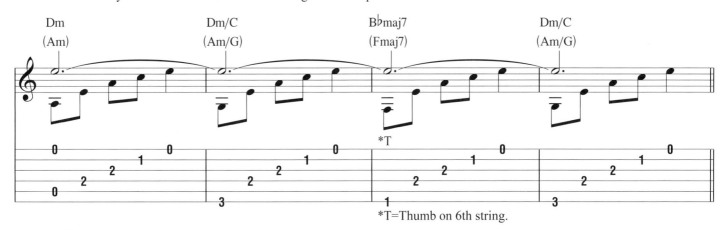

*T=Thumb on 6th string.

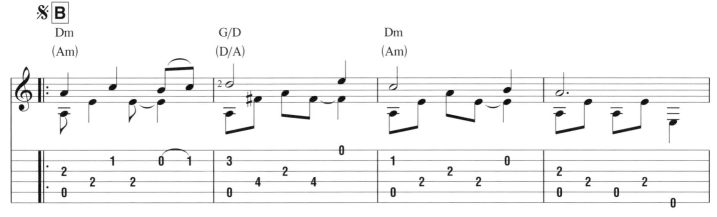

Copyright © 2004 MYRICA MUSIC, INC.
This arrangement Copyright © 2020 MYRICA MUSIC, INC.
All Rights in the U.S. and Canada Administered by UNIVERSAL - SONGS OF POLYGRAM INTERNATIONAL, INC.
All Rights Reserved   Used by Permission

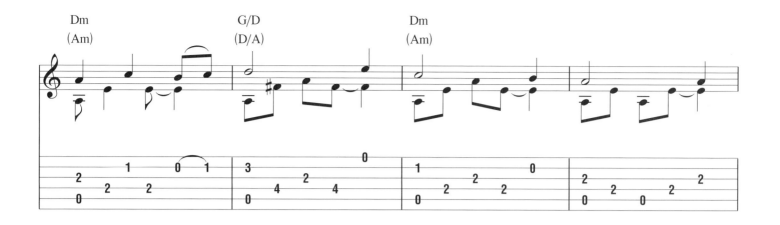

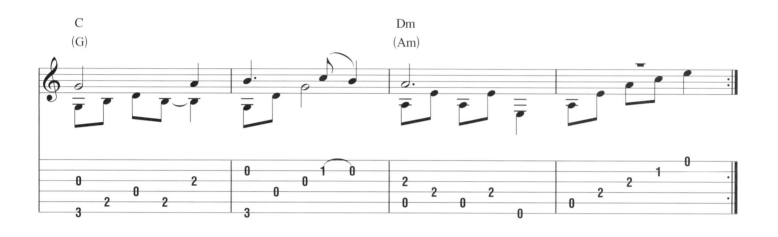

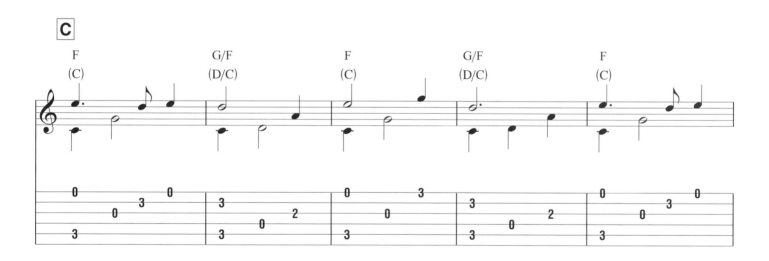

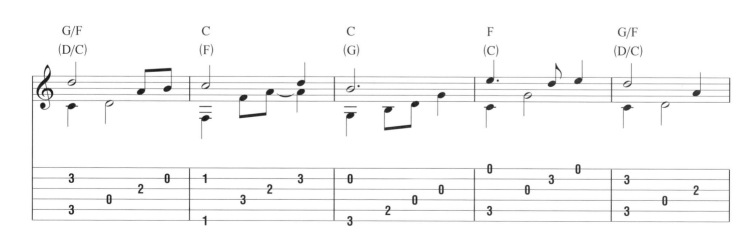

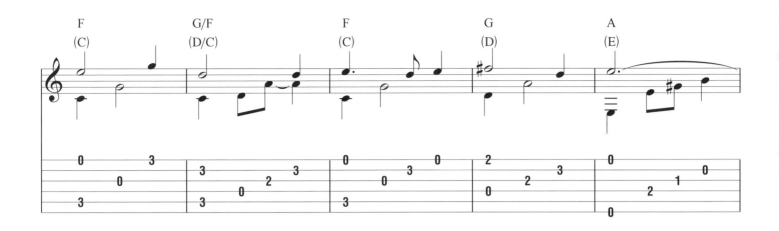

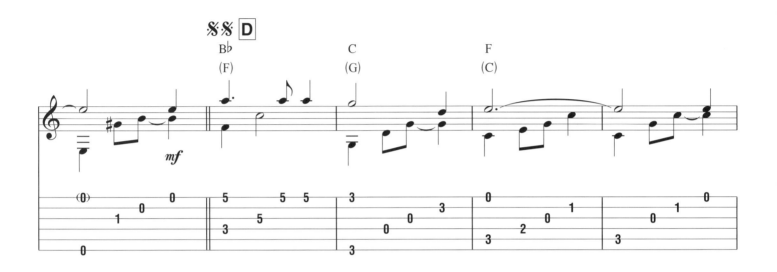

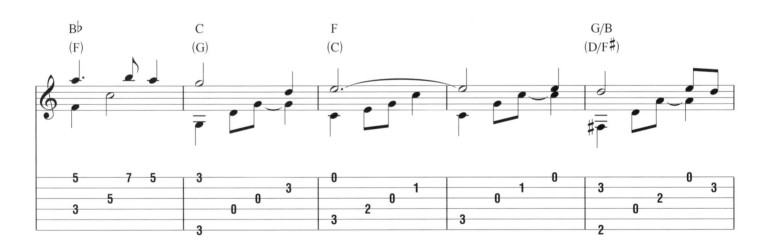

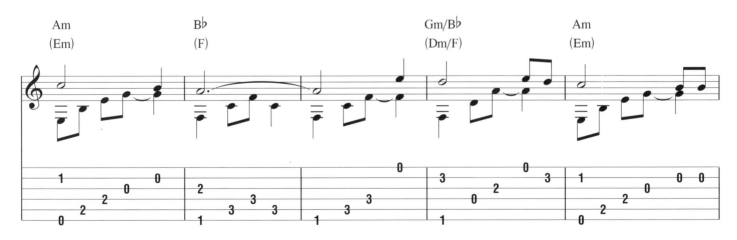

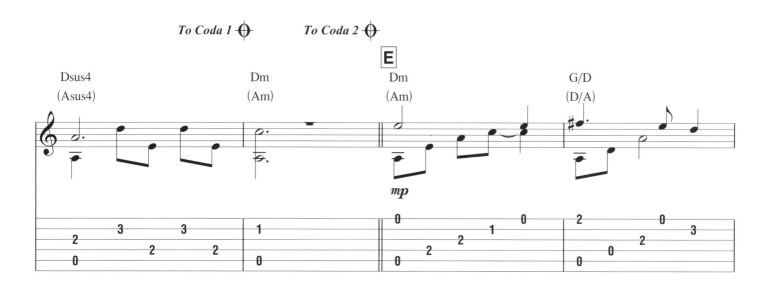

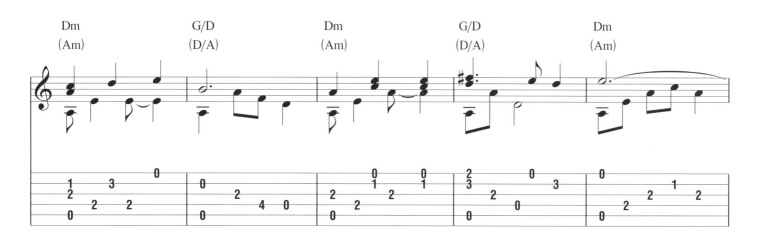

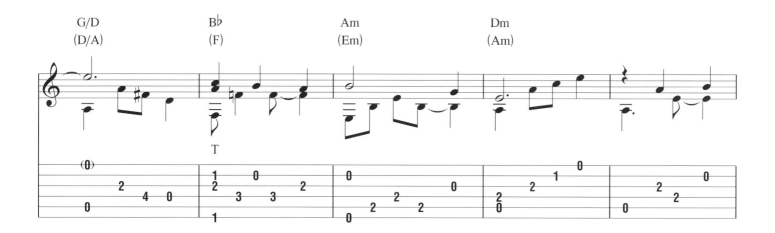

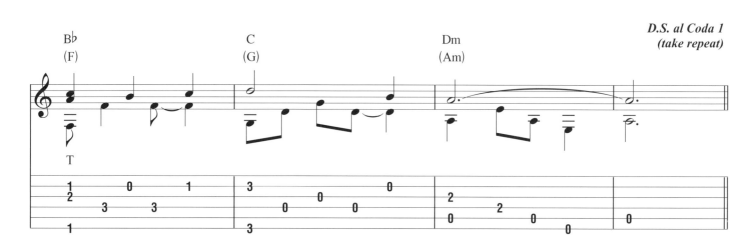

from **KINGDOM HEARTS**
Dearly Beloved
Music by Yoko Shimomura

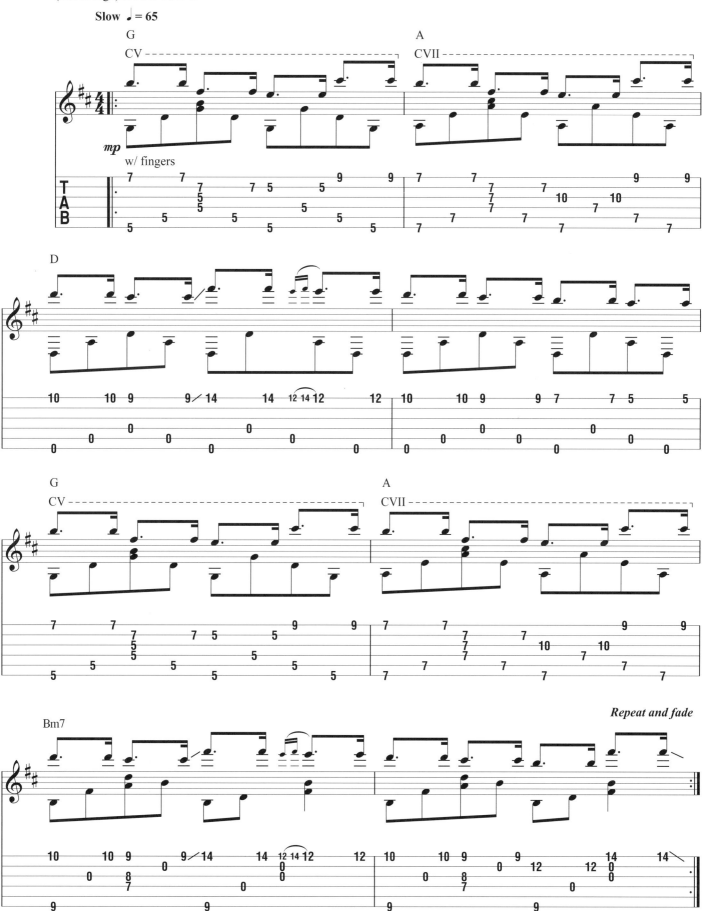

© 2003 Walt Disney Music Company
All Rights Reserved. Used by Permission.

27

Don't Forget

Words and Music by Toby Fox

Copyright © 2018 Royal Sciences LLC (administered by Materia Collective LLC)
This arrangement Copyright © 2020 Royal Sciences LLC (administered by Materia Collective LLC)
All Rights Reserved   Used by Permission

Elder Scrolls: Oblivion

By Jeremy Soule

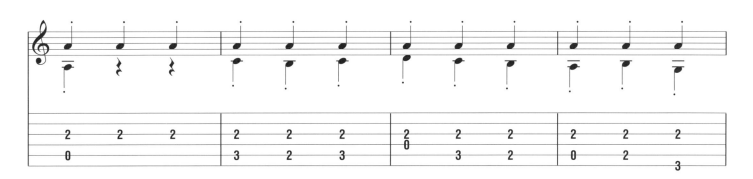

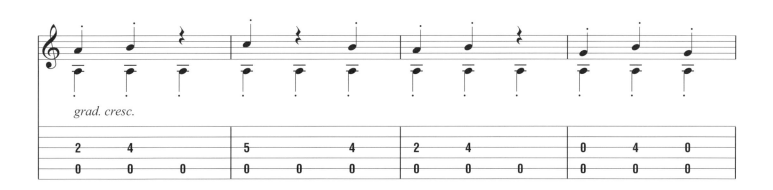

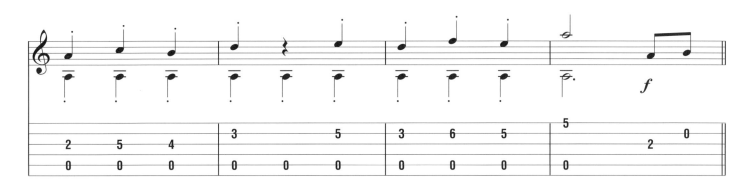

Copyright © 1994 Electronic Arts Music, Electronic Arts Inc. and Kobalt Music Copyrights SARL
This arrangement Copyright © 2020 Electronic Arts Music, Electronic Arts Inc. and Kobalt Music Copyrights SARL
All Rights Administered Worldwide by Kobalt Songs Music Publishing
All Rights Reserved   Used by Permission

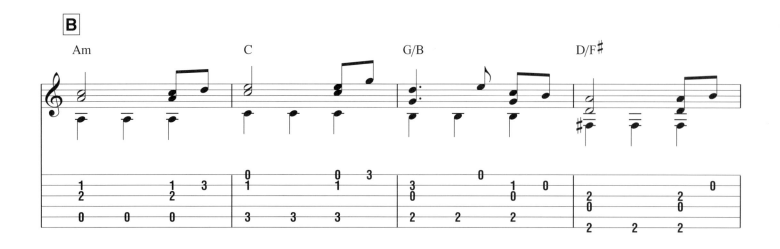

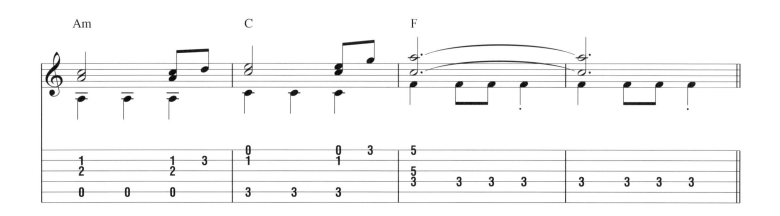

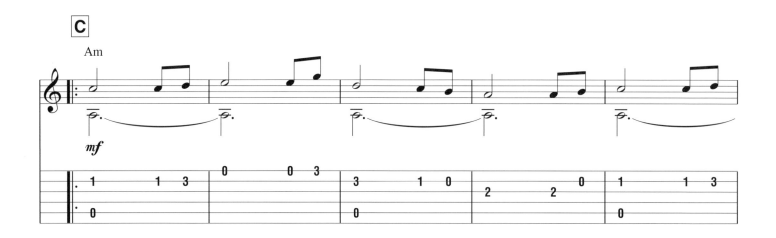

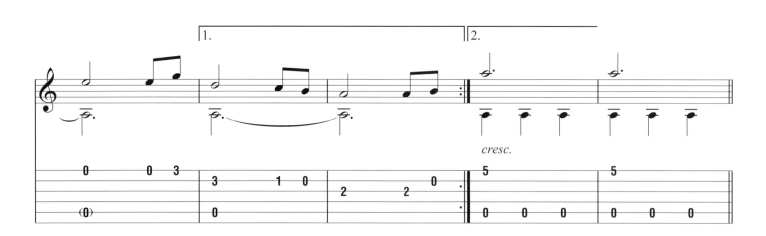

D

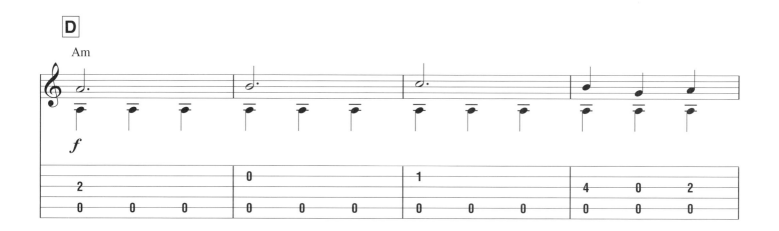

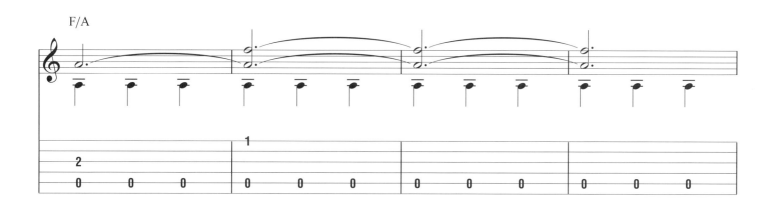

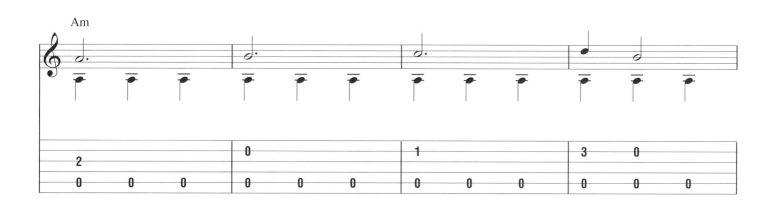

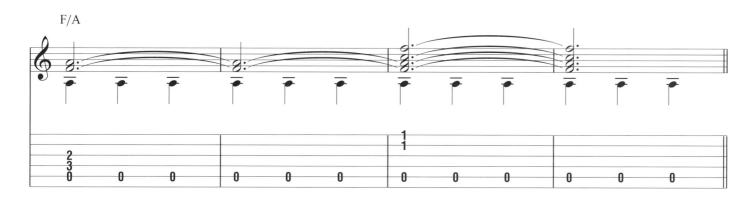

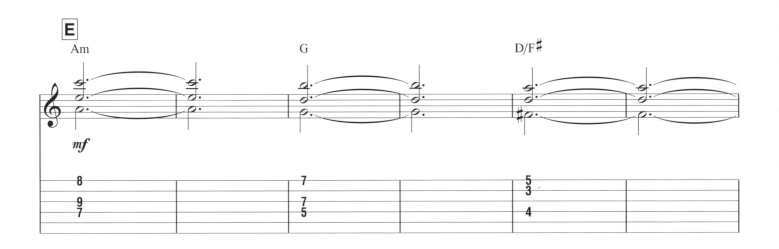

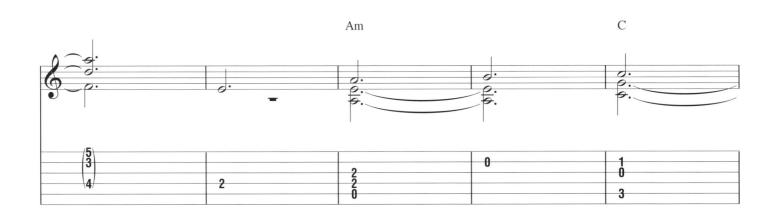

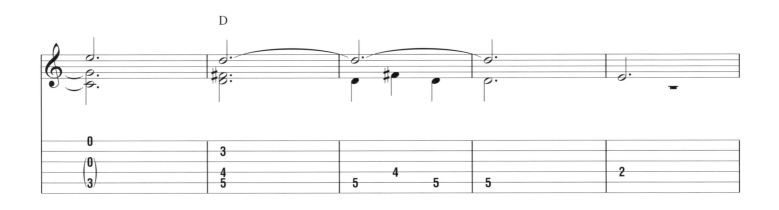

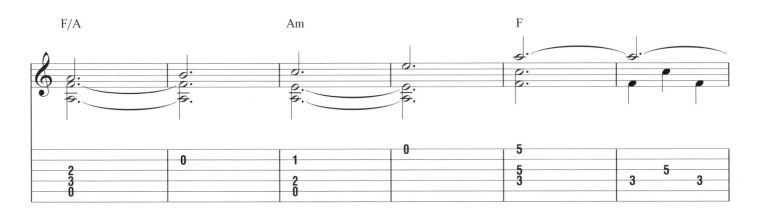

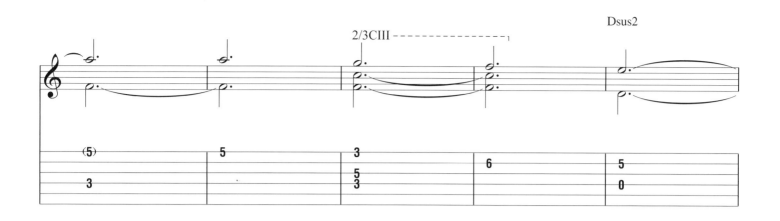

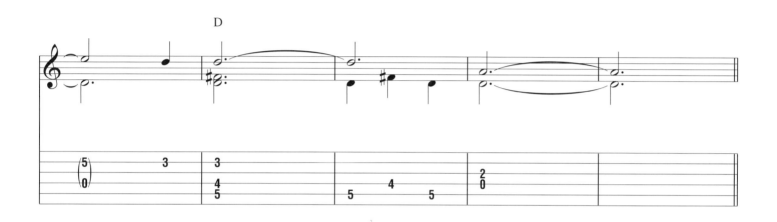

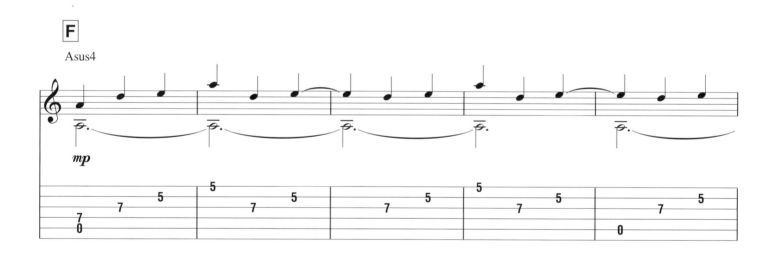

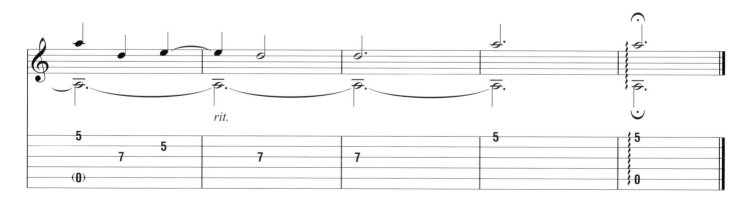

from FINAL FANTASY VIII

Eyes on Me

Music by Nobuo Uematsu
Lyrics by Kako Someya

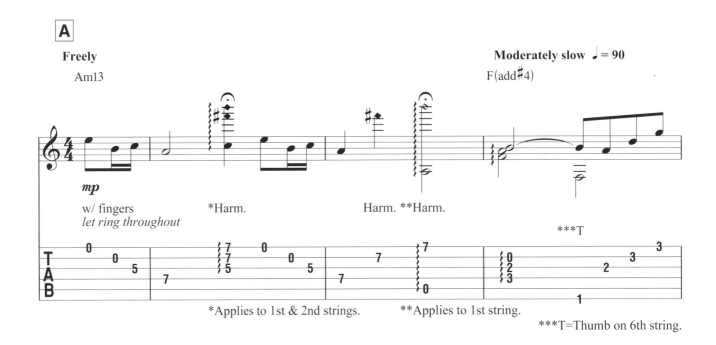

*Applies to 1st & 2nd strings.   **Applies to 1st string.

***T=Thumb on 6th string.

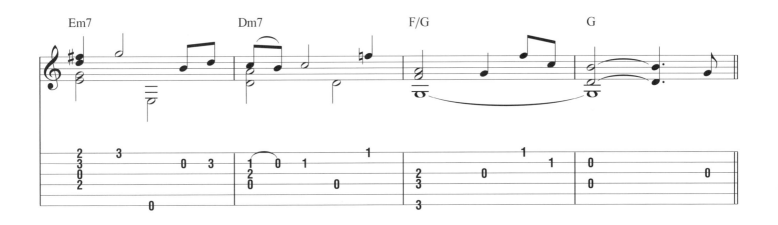

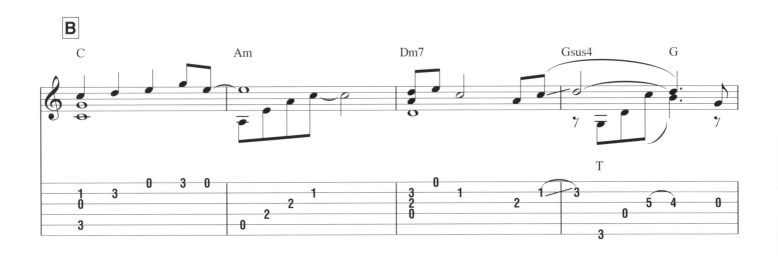

© 1999 SQUARE ENIX CO. LTD.
This arrangement Copyright © 2020 SQUARE ENIX CO. LTD.
All Rights in the U.S. and Canada Administered by WC MUSIC CORP.
All Rights Reserved   Used by Permission

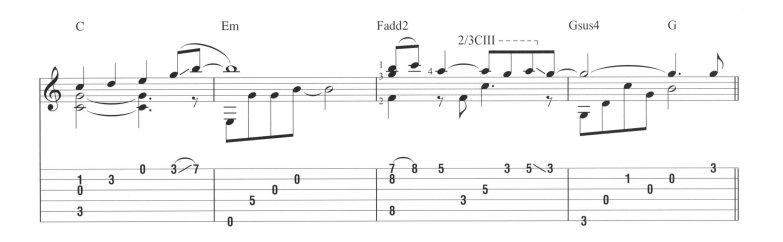

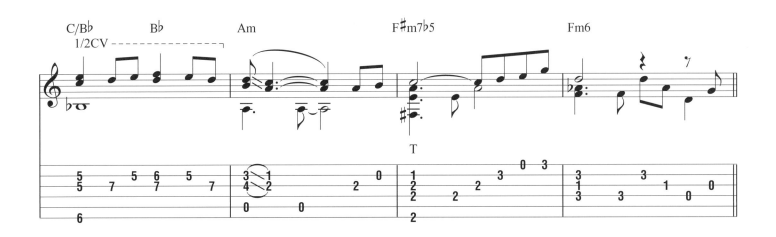

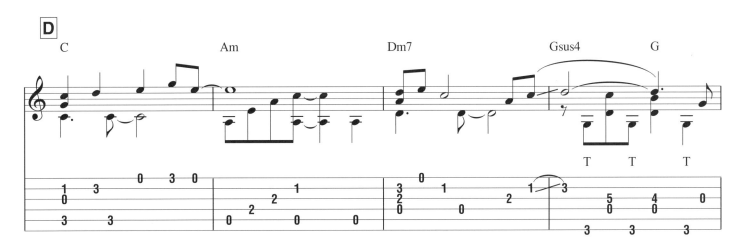

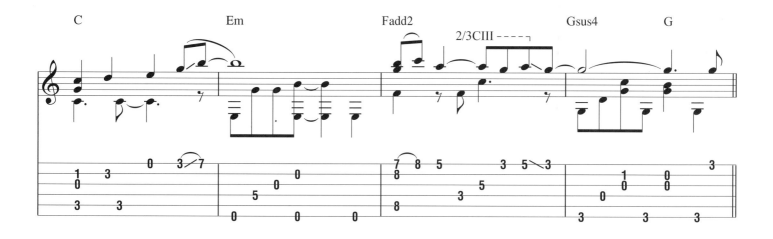

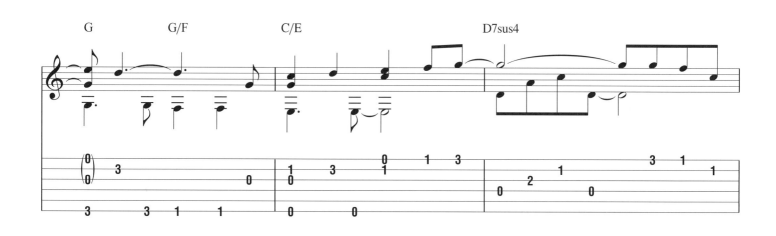

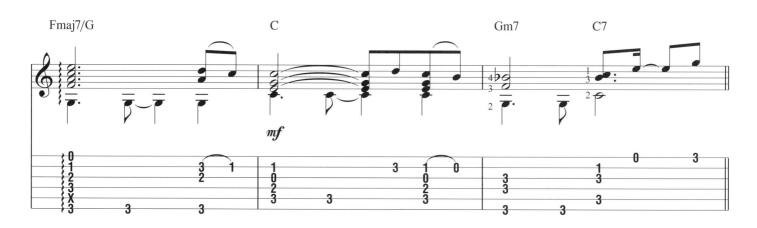

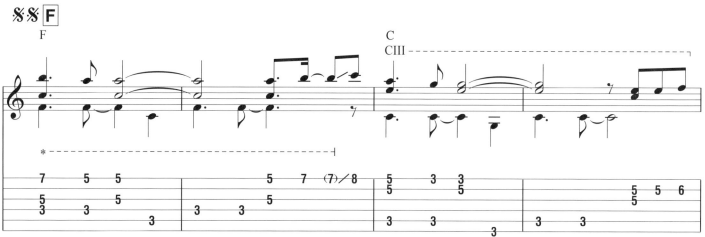

*Barre top 3 strings w/ ring finger at 5th fret.

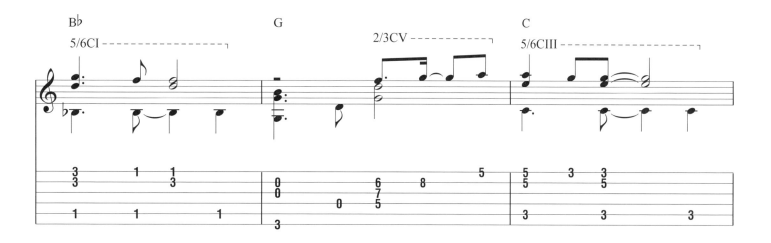

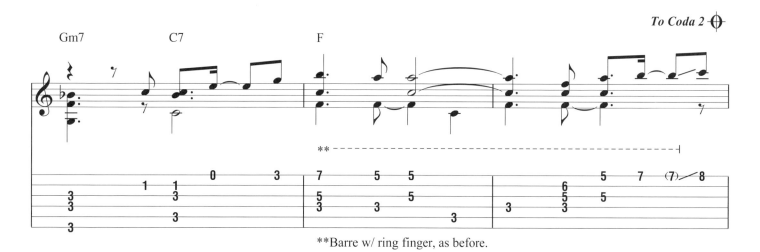

**Barre w/ ring finger, as before.

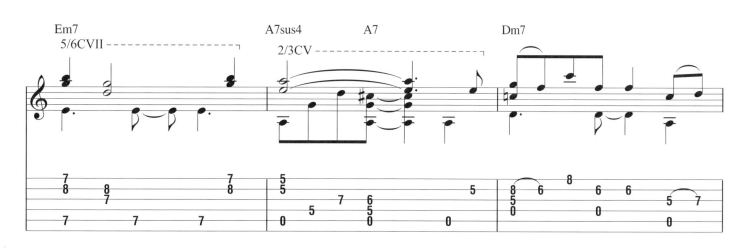

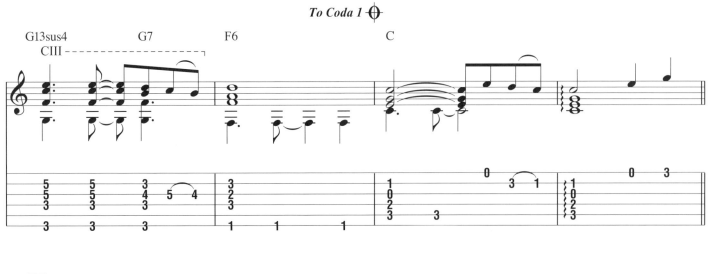

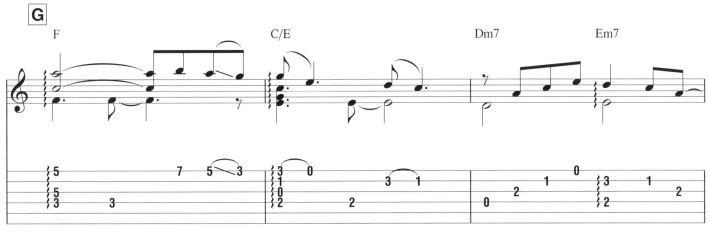

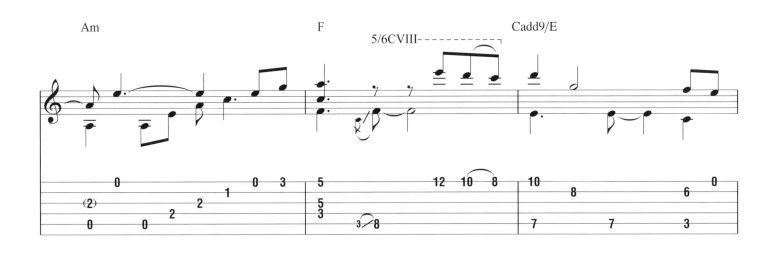

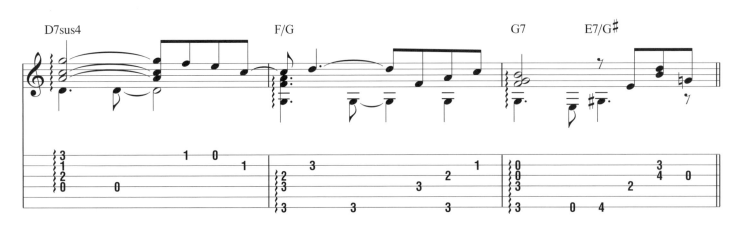

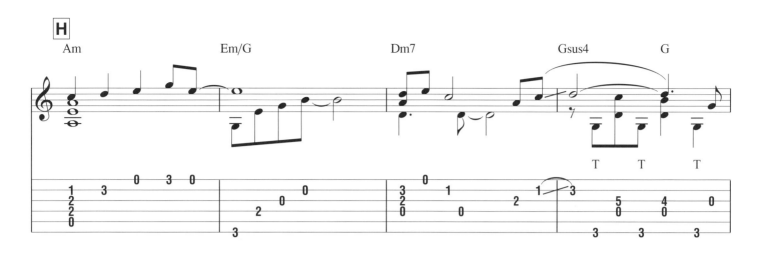

D.S. al Coda 1

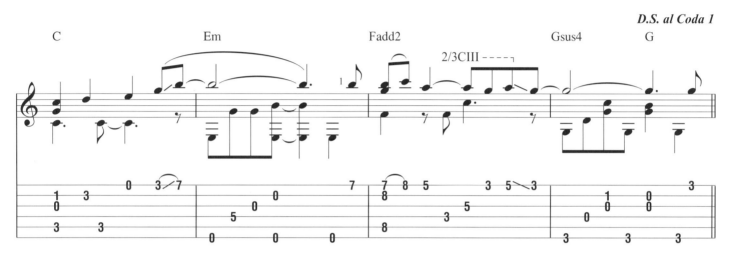

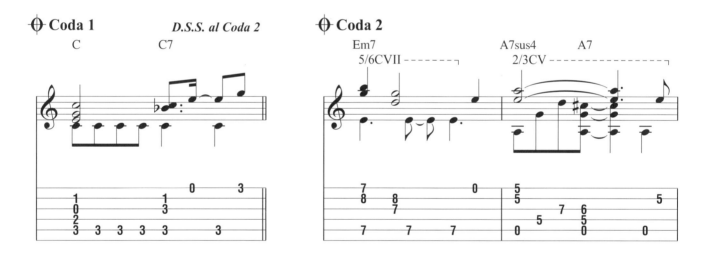

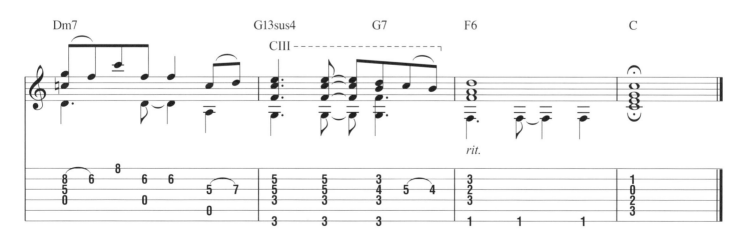

Theme from Fallout® 4

Composed by Inon Zur

Copyright © 2015 Bethesda Softworks LLC, a Zenimax Media company
This arrangement Copyright © 2020 Bethesda Softworks LLC, a Zenimax Media company
All Rights Reserved
No portion of this sheet music may be reproduced or transmitted in any form
or by any means without written permission from Bethesda Softworks LLC.

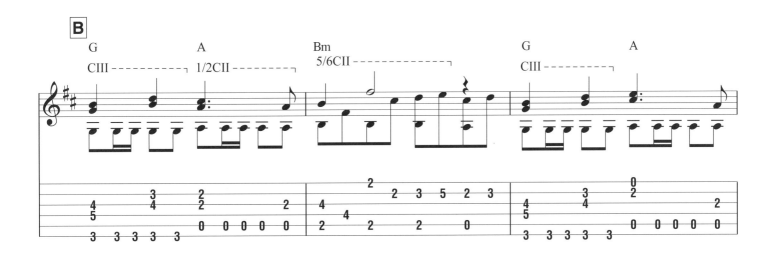

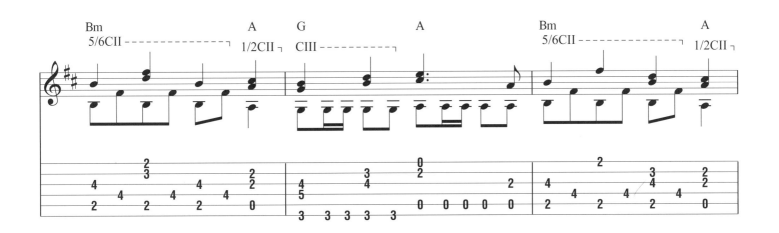

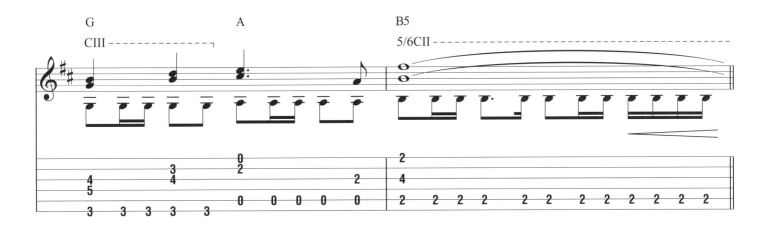

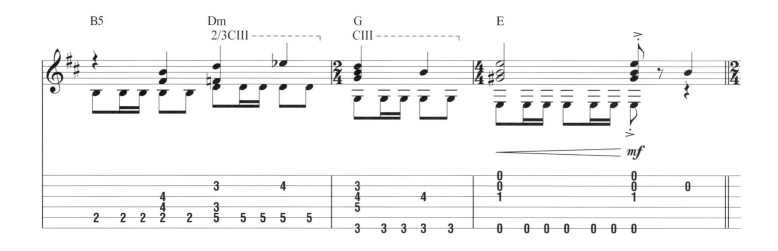

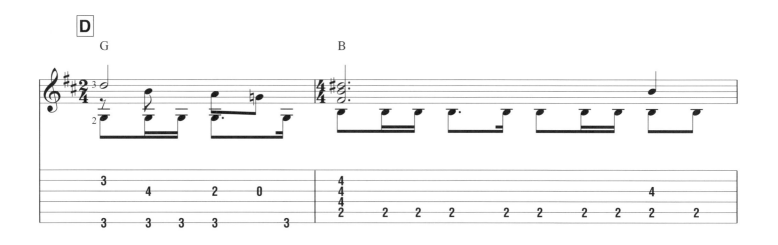

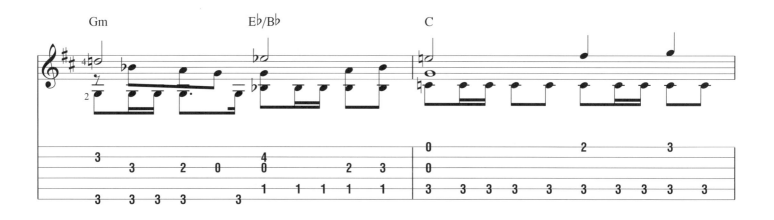

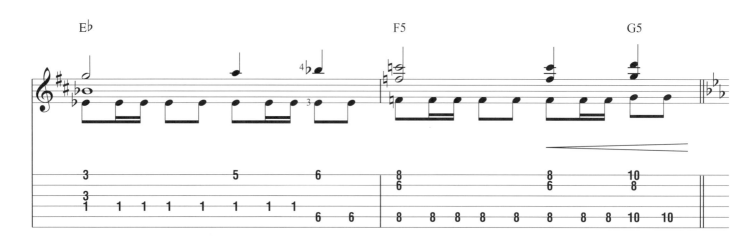

*Strum w/ thumb.

Main Theme (Final Fantasy I)

By Nobuo Uematsu

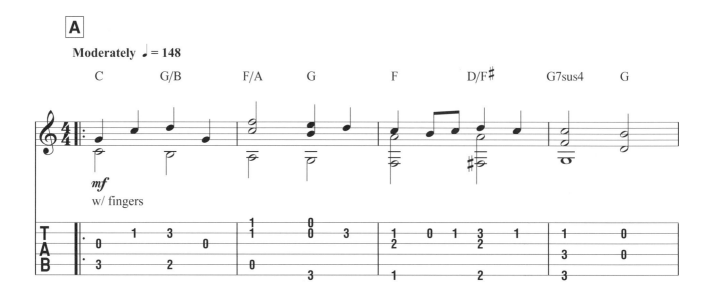

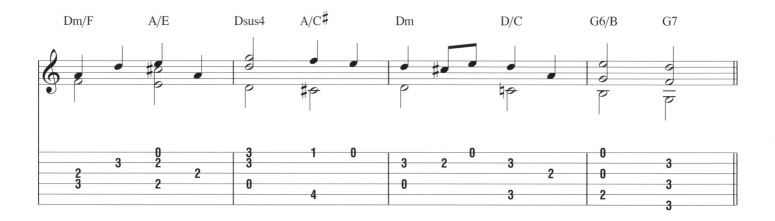

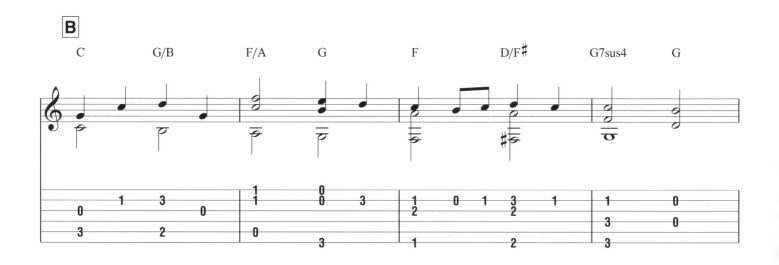

© 1987 SQUARE ENIX CO. LTD.
This arrangement Copyright © 2020 SQUARE ENIX CO. LTD.
All Rights in the U.S. and Canada Administered by WC MUSIC CORP.
All Rights Reserved   Used by Permission

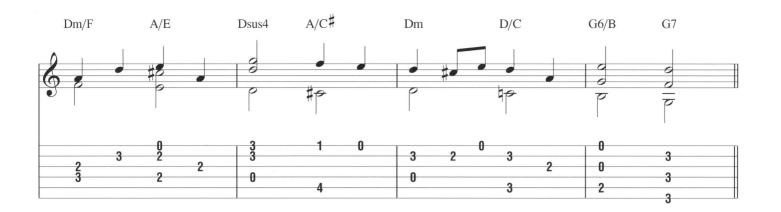

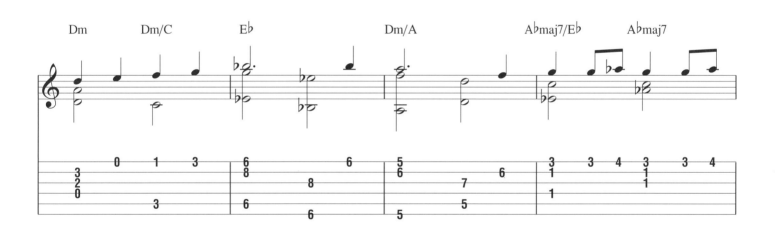

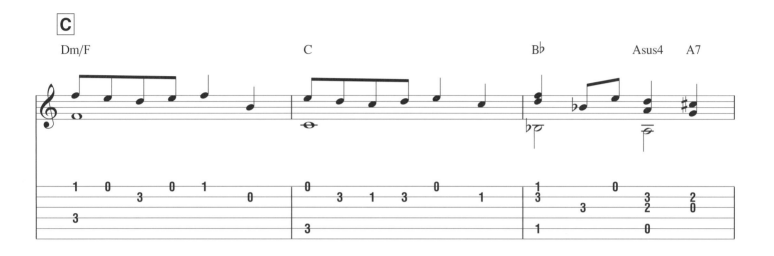

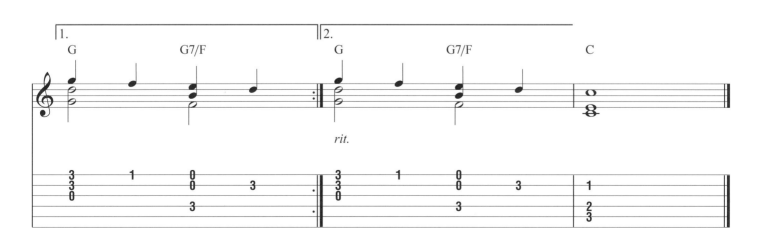

Main Theme (Final Fantasy VII)

By Nobuo Uematsu

© 1997 SQUARE ENIX CO. LTD.
This arrangement Copyright © 2020 SQUARE ENIX CO. LTD.
All Rights in the U.S. and Canada Administered by WC MUSIC CORP.
All Rights Reserved   Used by Permission

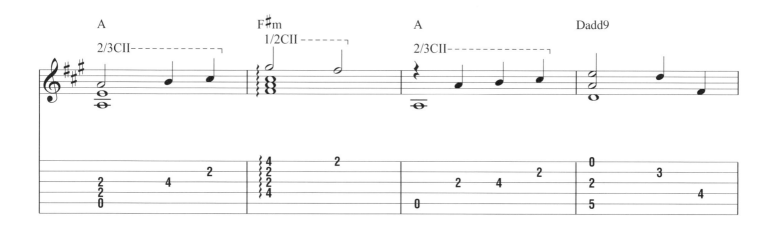

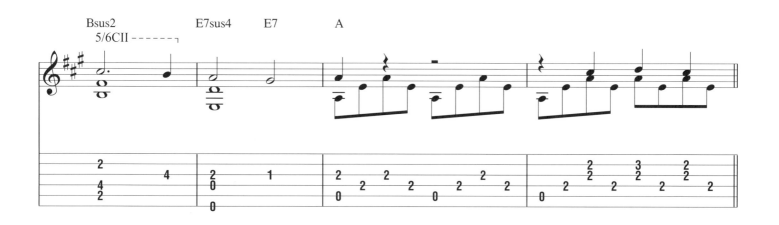

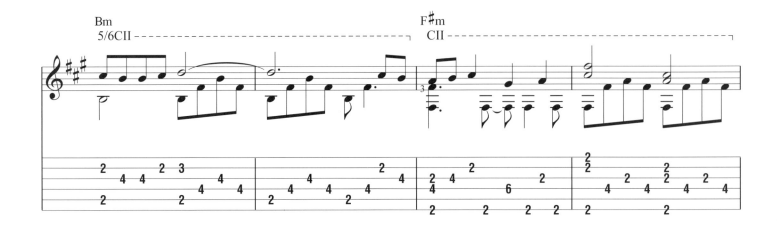

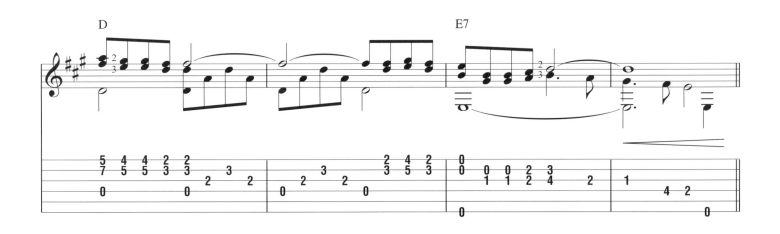

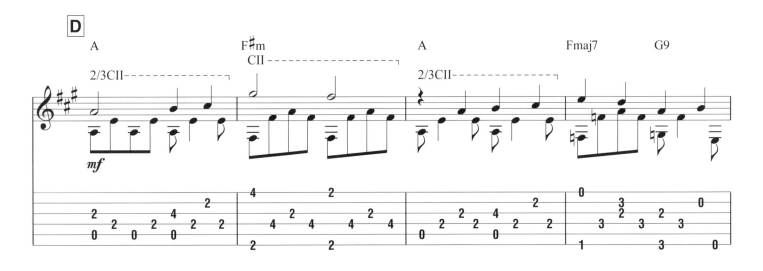

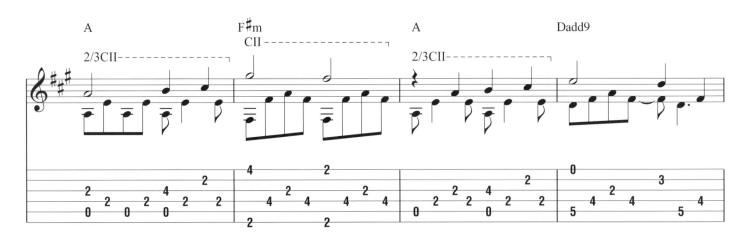

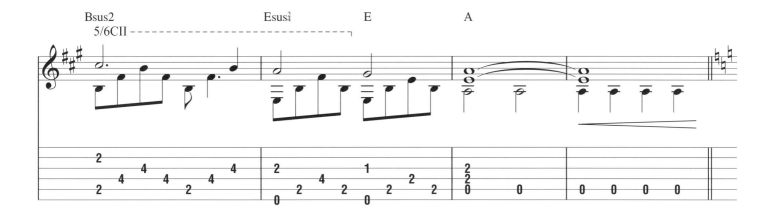

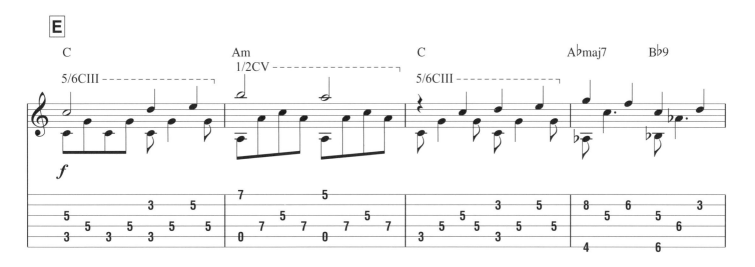

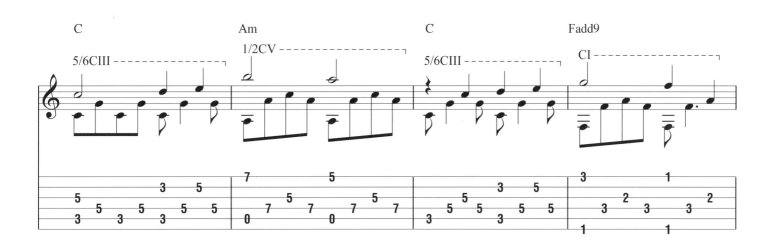

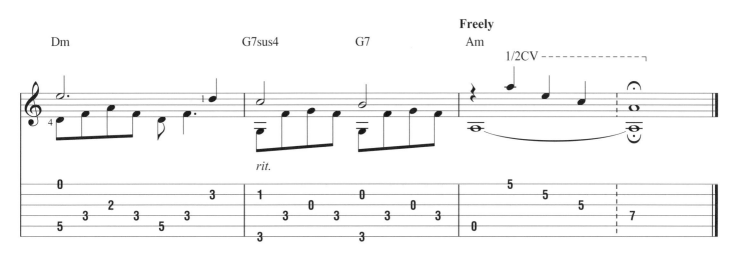

from UNDERTALE®
Megalovania
Music by Toby Fox

Double Drop D tuning:
(low to high) D-A-D-G-B-D

A

Moderately ♩ = 110

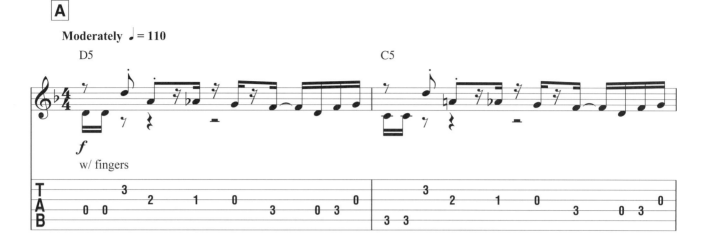

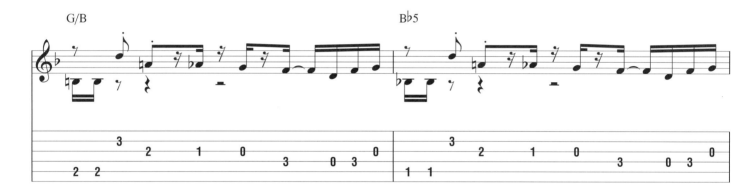

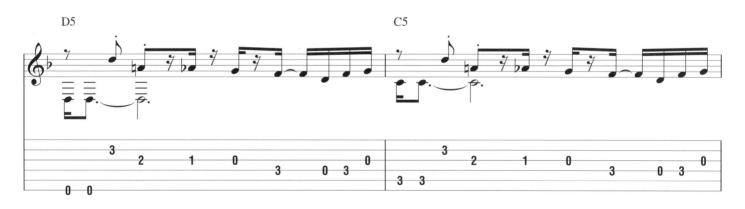

Copyright © 2015 Royal Sciences LLC (administered by Materia Collective LLC)
This arrangement Copyright © 2020 Royal Sciences LLC (administered by Materia Collective LLC)
All Rights Reserved   Used by Permission

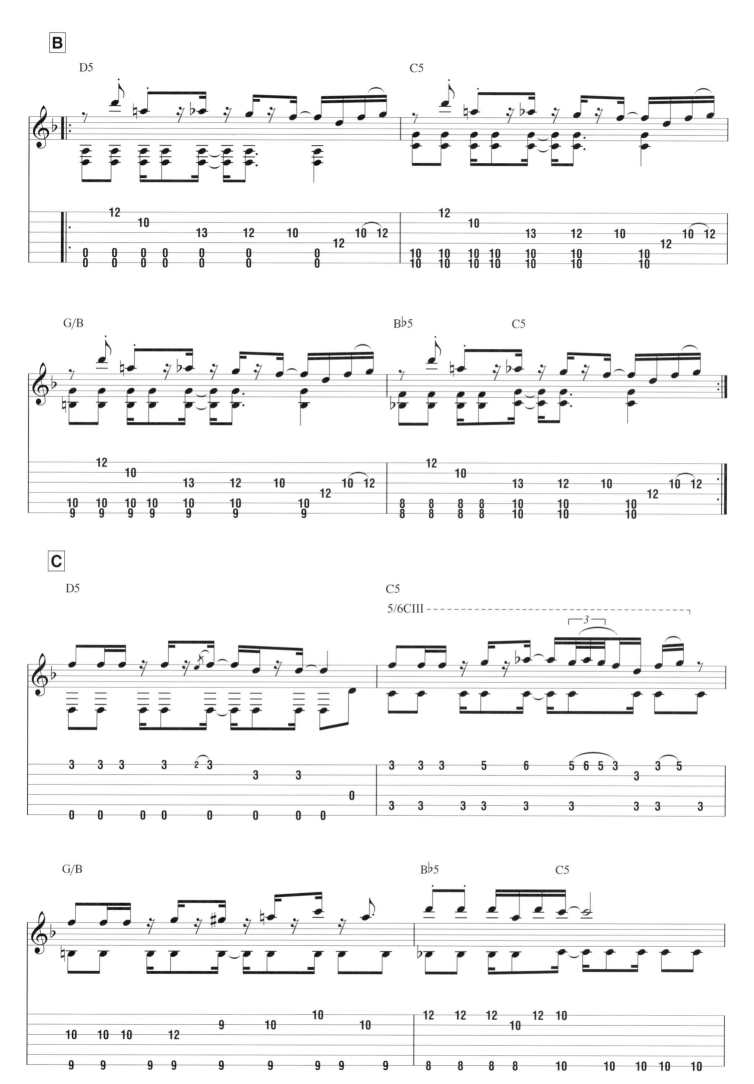

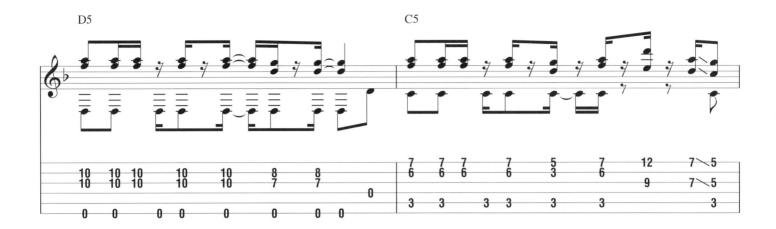

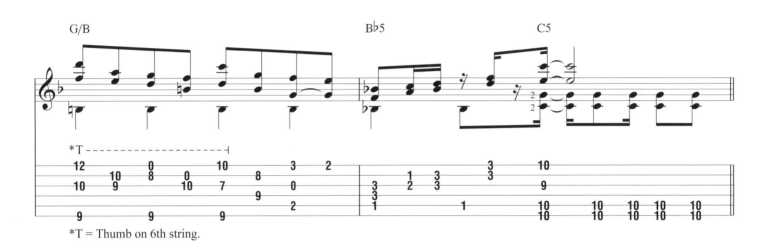

*T = Thumb on 6th string.

D

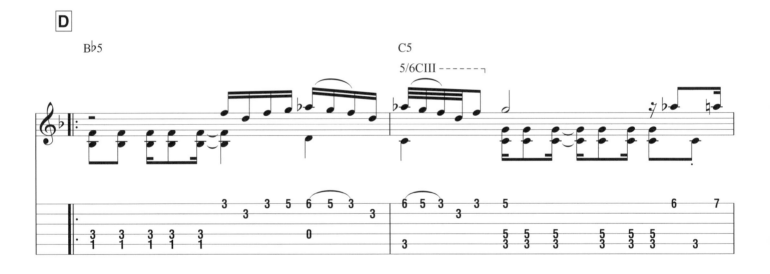

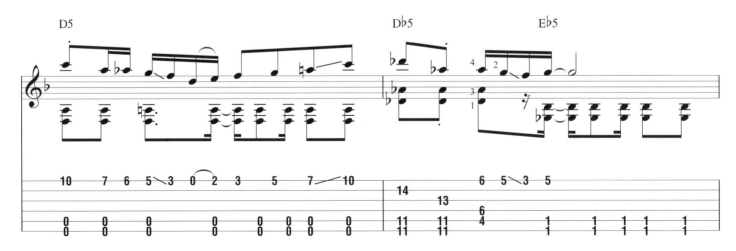

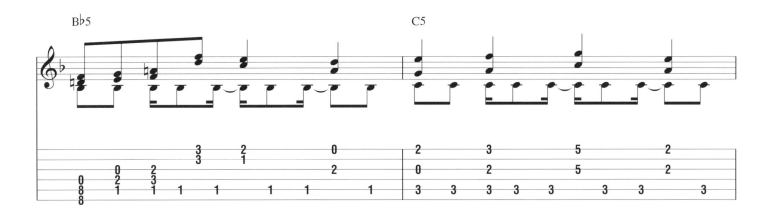

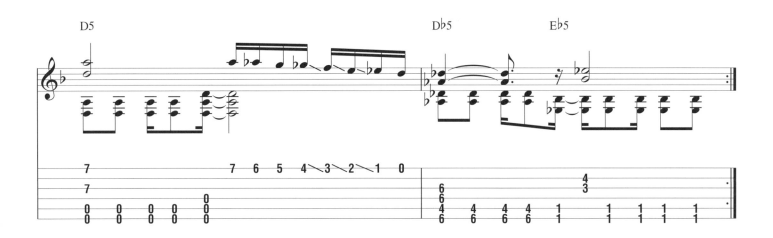

E

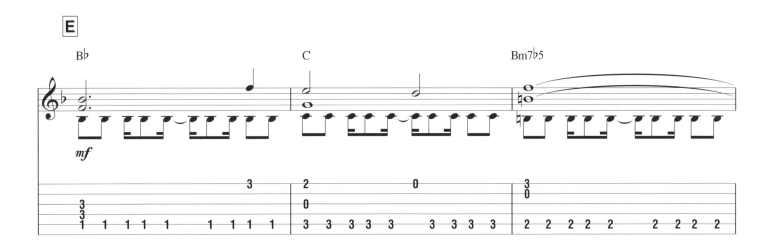

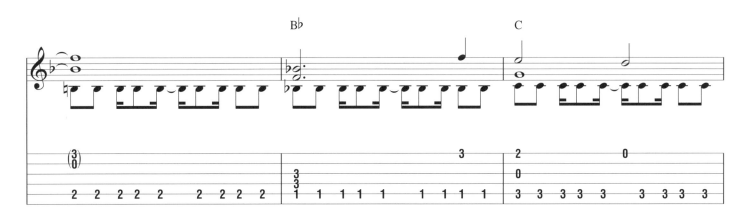

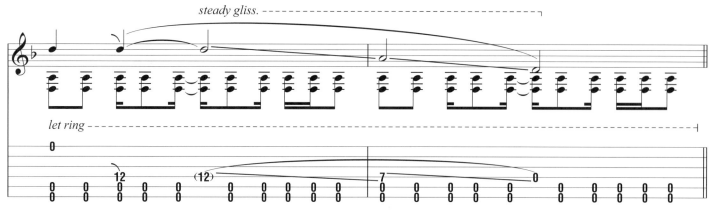

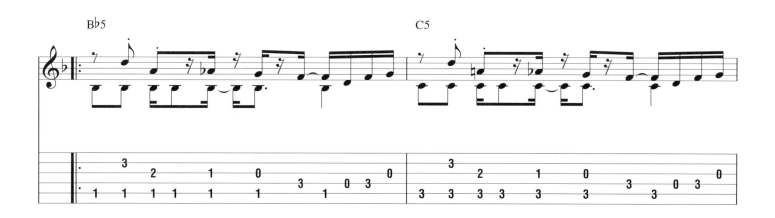

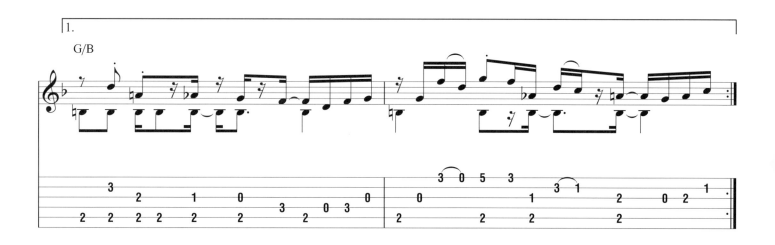

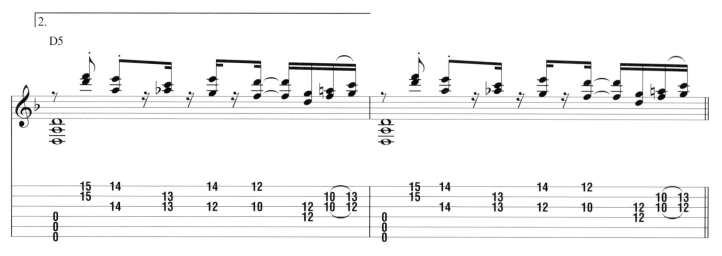

F

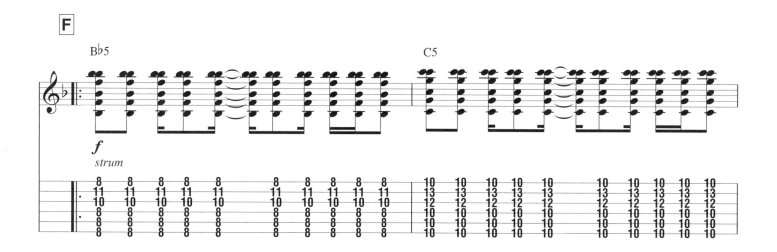

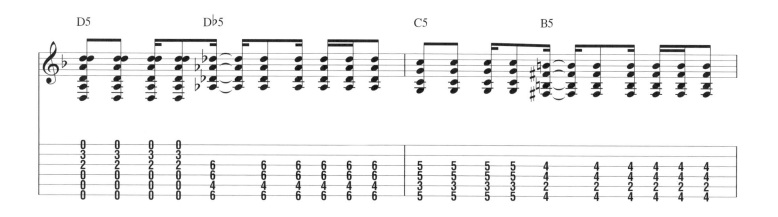

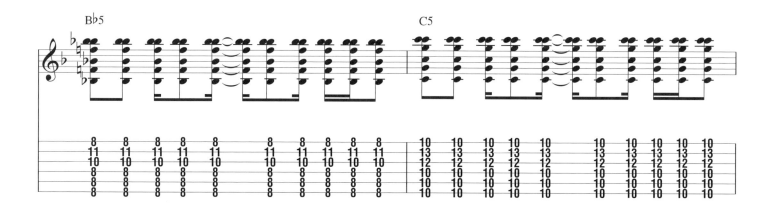

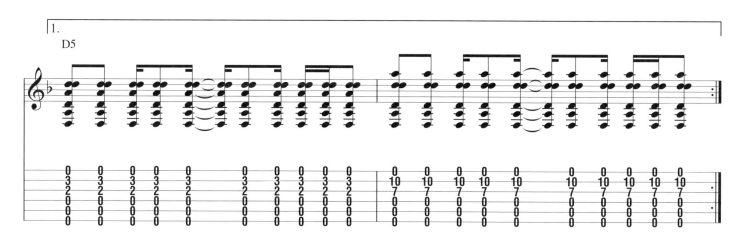

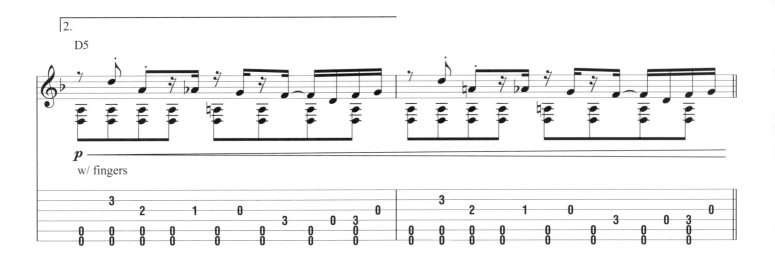

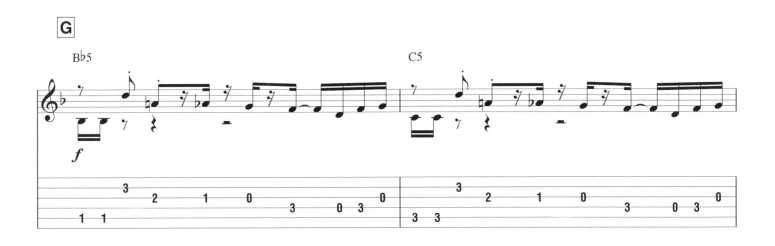

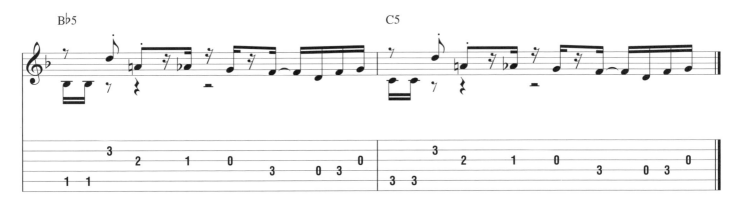

Sadness and Sorrow

By Purojekuto Musashi

Copyright © 2002 TV Tokyo Music, Inc.
This arrangement Copyright © 2020 TV Tokyo Music, Inc.
All Rights Administered by Sony/ATV Music Publishing LLC, 424 Church Street, Suite 1200, Nashville, TN 37219
International Copyright Secured   All Rights Reserved

from **MINECRAFT**
Minecraft: Sweden
By Daniel Rosenfeld

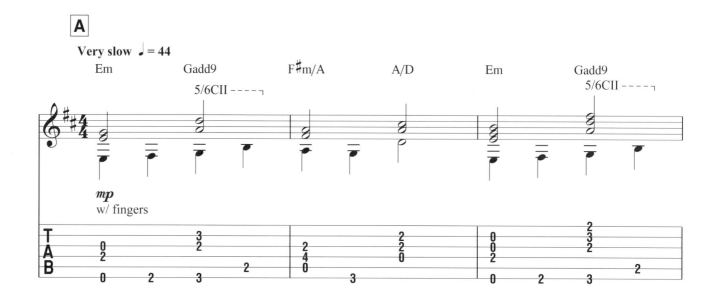

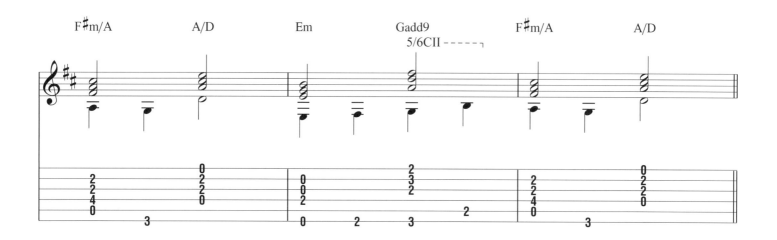

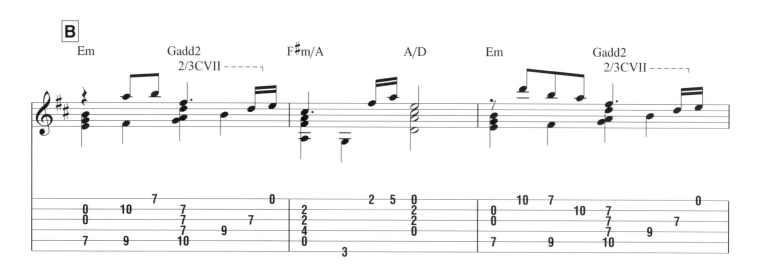

Copyright © 2011 Tunecore Digital Music
This arrangement Copyright © 2020 Tunecore Digital Music
All Rights Reserved   Used by Permission

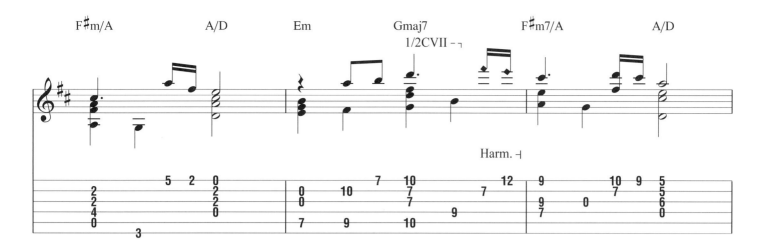

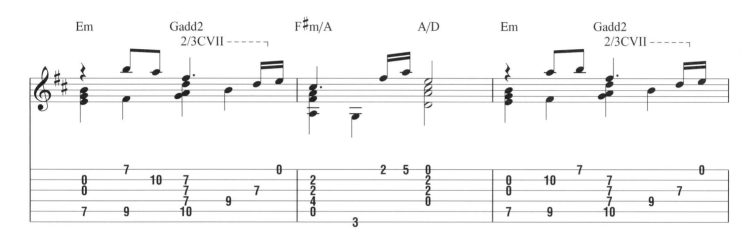

*Refers to upstemmed note only.

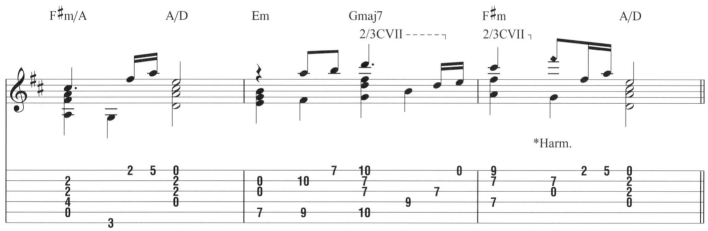

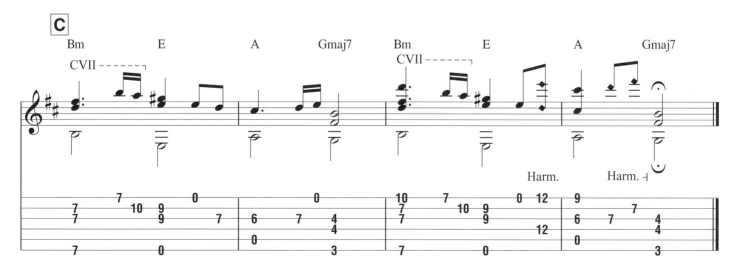

from **RED DEAD REDEMPTION II**
That's the Way It Is
Words and Music by Daniel Lanois and Rocco DeLuca

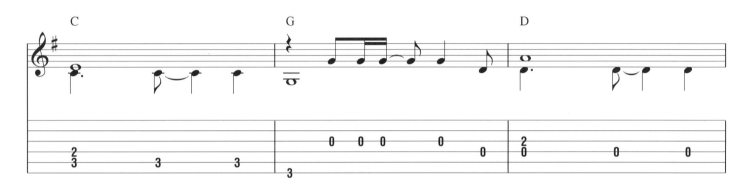

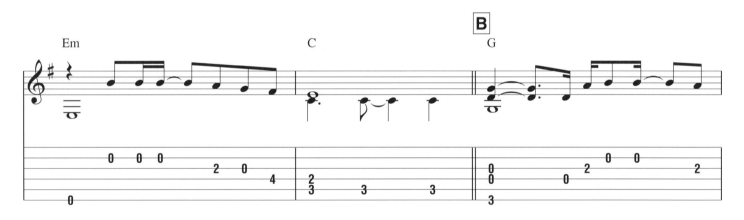

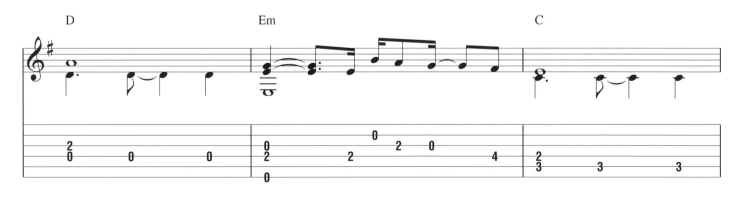

Copyright © 2018 Daniel Lanois Songs and Rockstar Games Entertainment
This arrangement Copyright © 2020 Daniel Lanois Songs and Rockstar Games Entertainment
All Rights for Daniel Lanois Songs Administered by Penny Farthing Music c/o Concord Music Publishing
All Rights for Rockstar Games Entertainment Administered Worldwide by Songs Of Kobalt Music Publishing
All Rights Reserved   Used by Permission

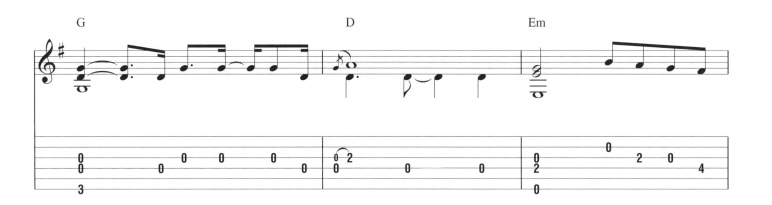

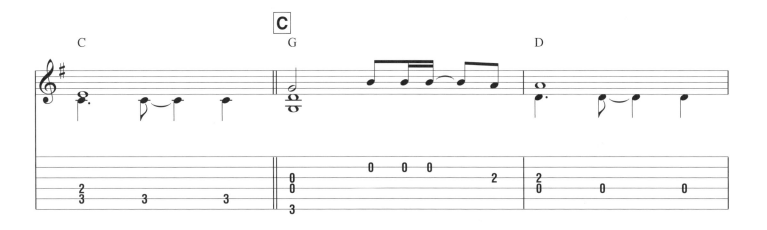

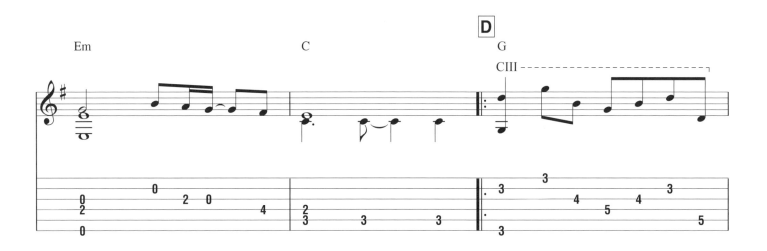

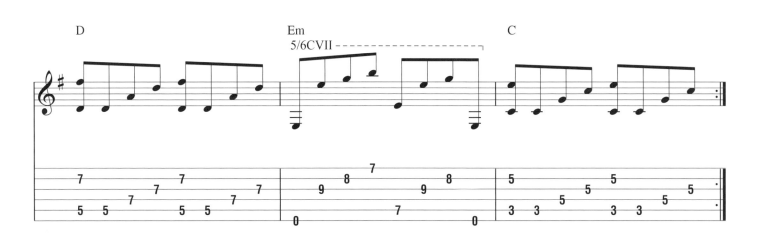

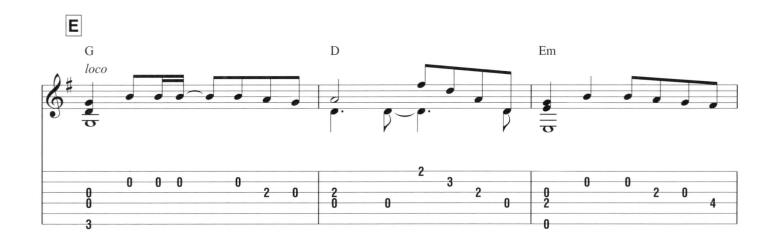

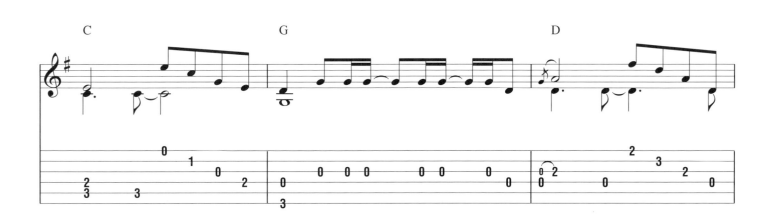

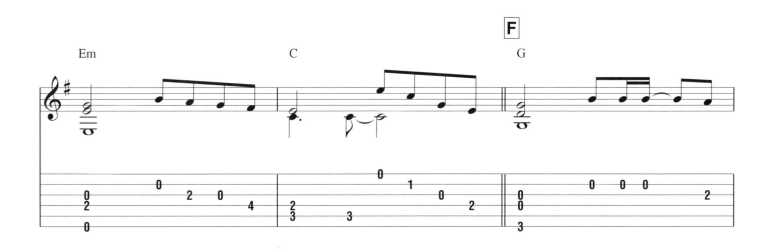

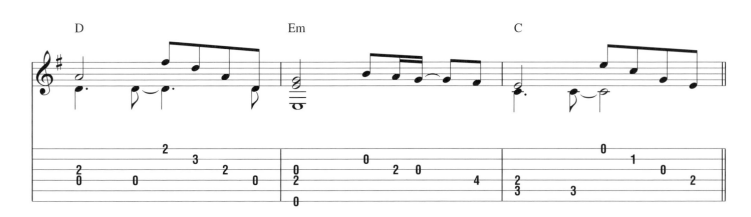

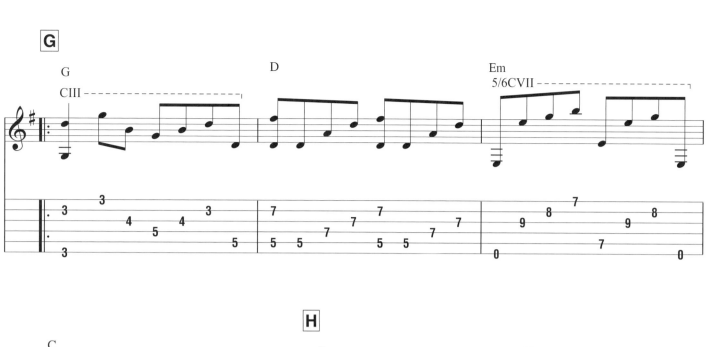

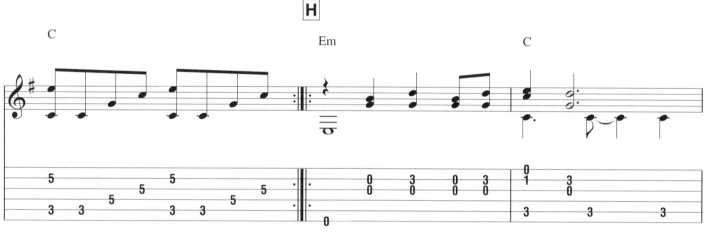

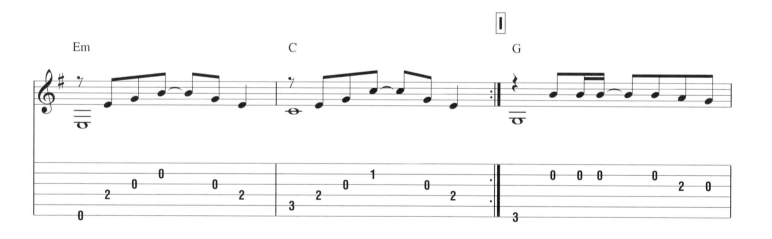

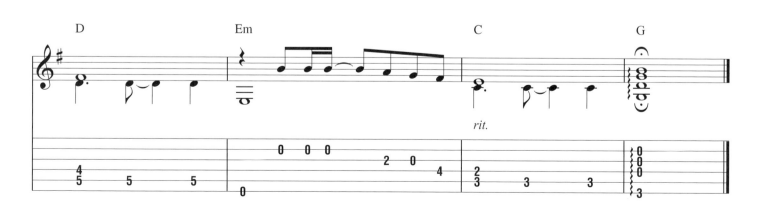

from **RED DEAD REDEMPTION II**
Unshaken

Words and Music by Daniel Lanois, Michael Archer and Rocco DeLuca

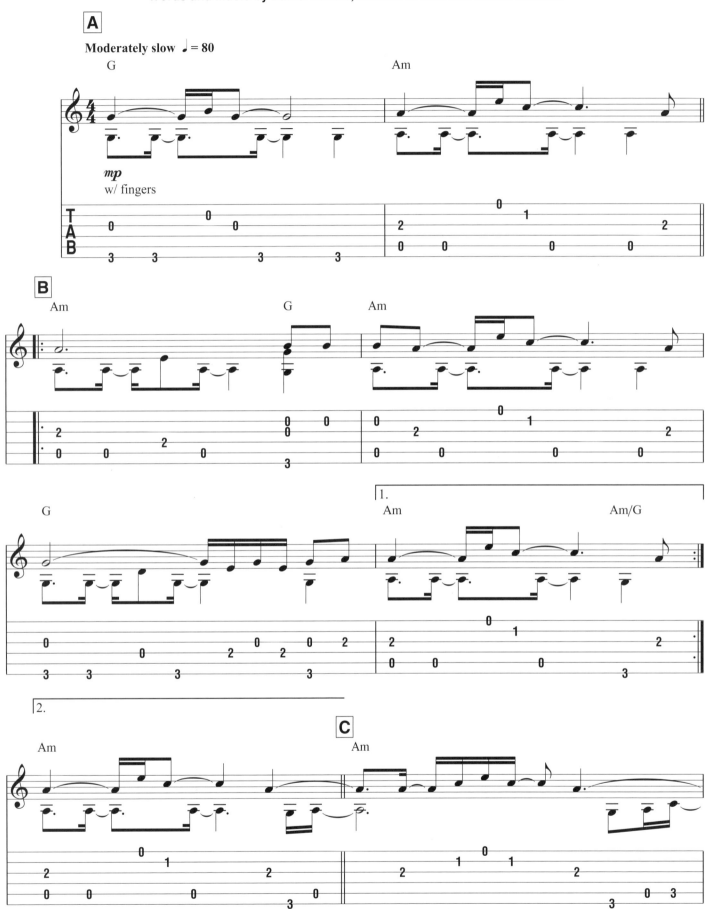

Copyright © 2018, 2019 Daniel Lanois Songs, Universal - PolyGram International Publishing, Inc.,
Ah Choo Music Publishing and Rockstar Games Entertainment
This arrangement Copyright © 2020 Daniel Lanois Songs, Universal - PolyGram International Publishing, Inc.,
Ah Choo Music Publishing and Rockstar Games Entertainment
All Rights for Daniel Lanois Songs Administered by Penny Farthing Music c/o Concord Music Publishing
All Rights for Ah Choo Music Publishing Administered by Universal - PolyGram International Publishing, Inc.
All Rights for Rockstar Games Entertainment Administered Worldwide by Songs Of Kobalt Music Publishing
All Rights Reserved   Used by Permission

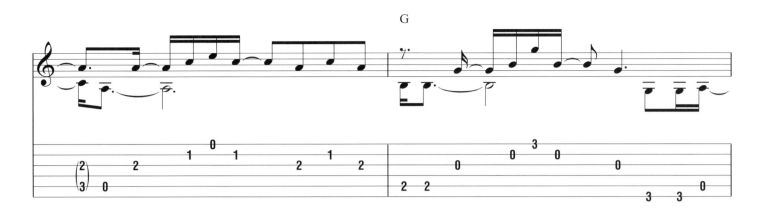

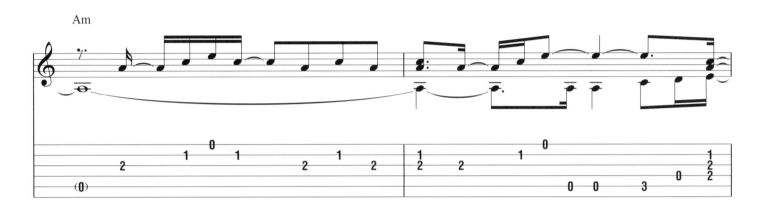

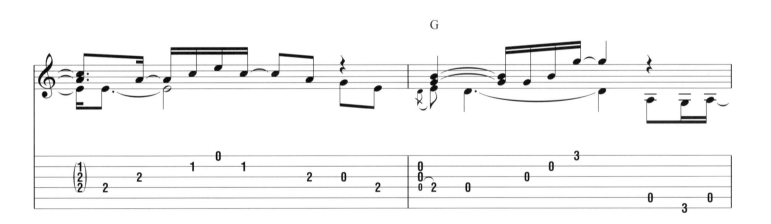

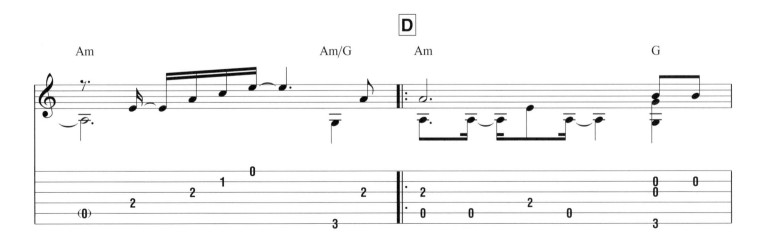

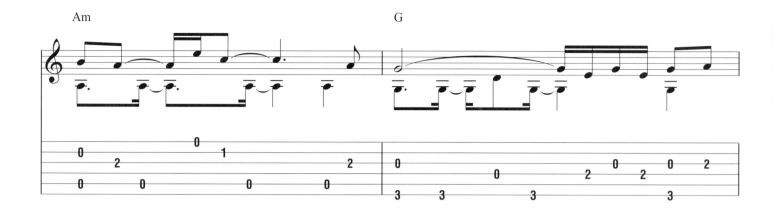

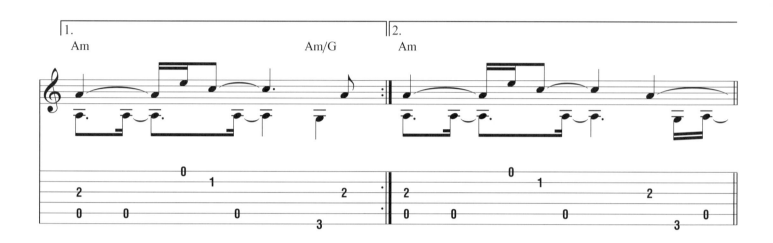

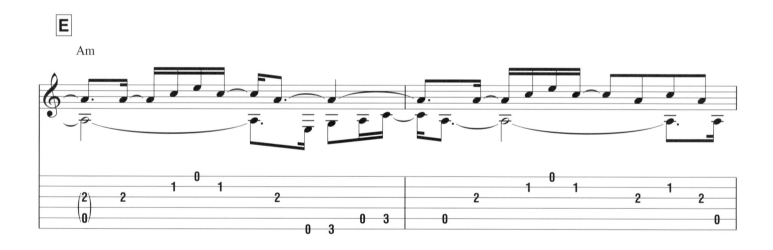

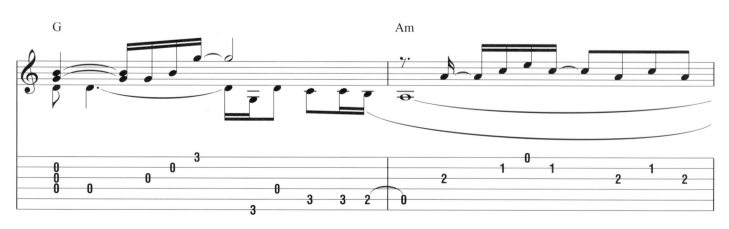

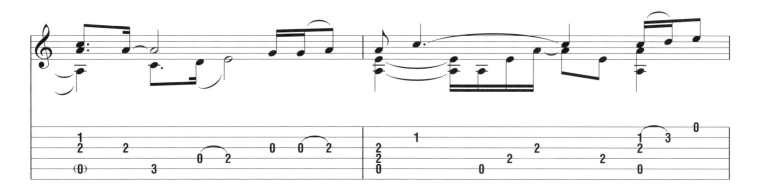

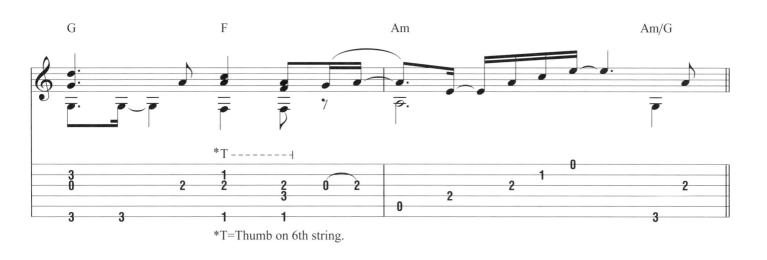

*T = Thumb on 6th string.

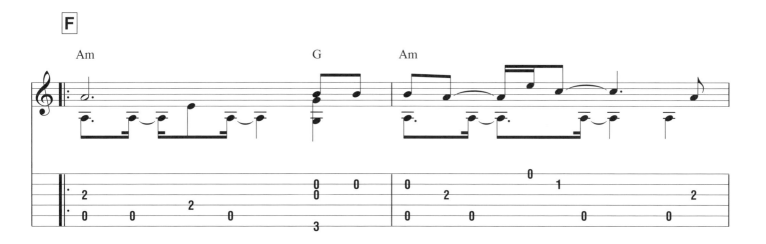

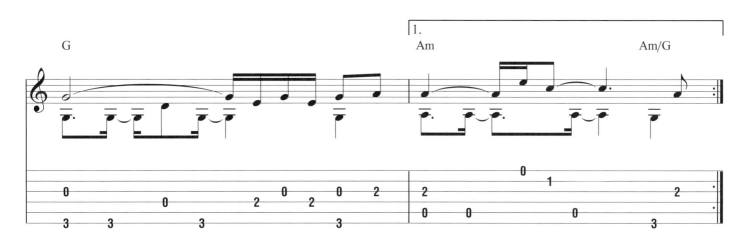

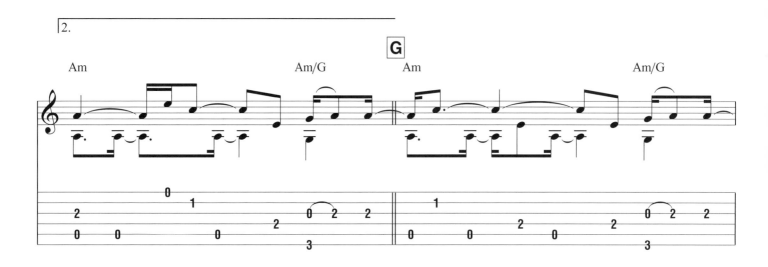

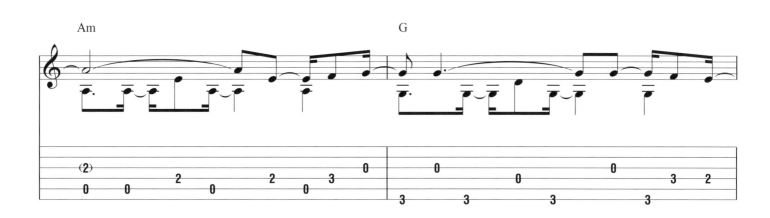

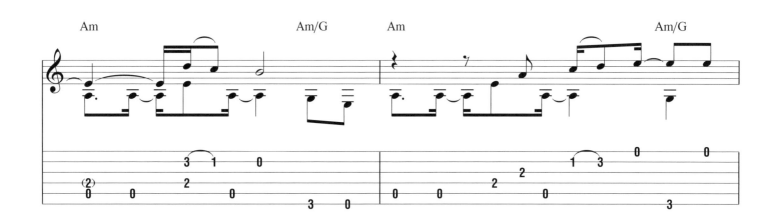

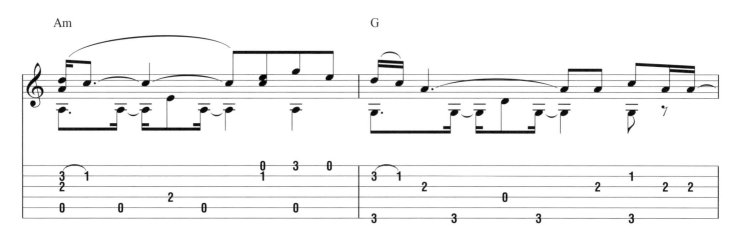

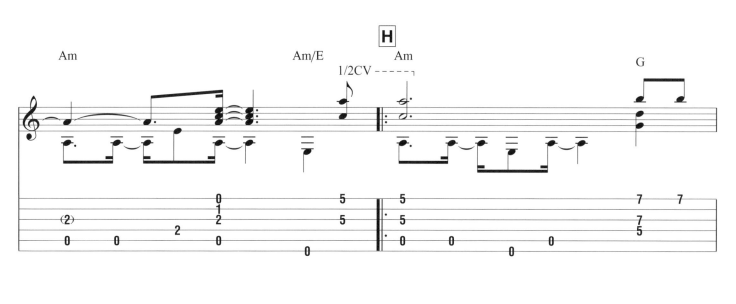

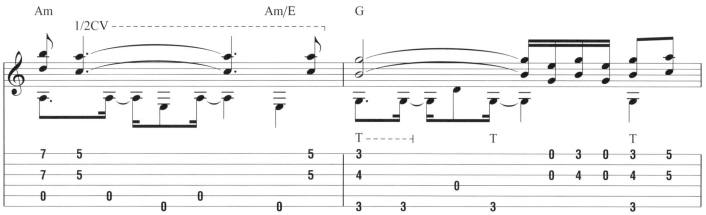

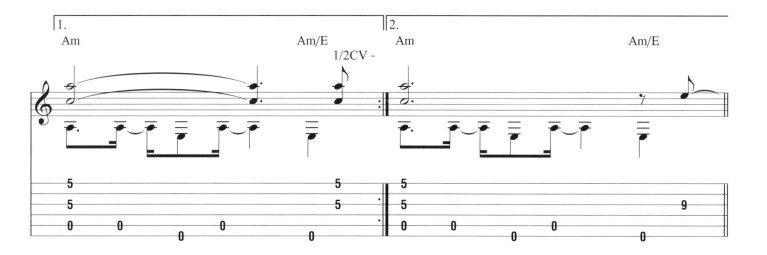

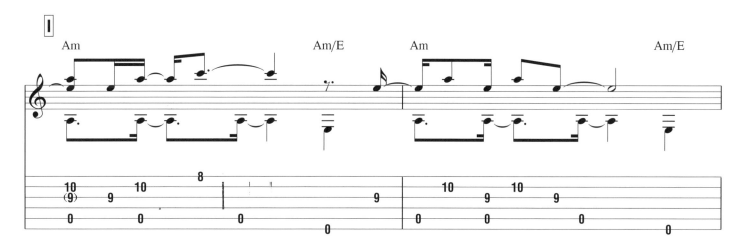

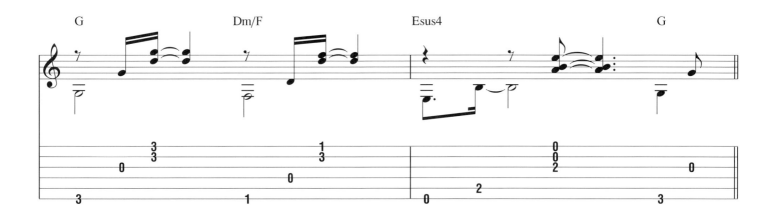

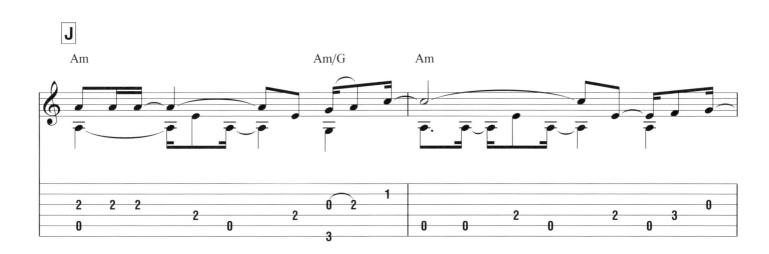

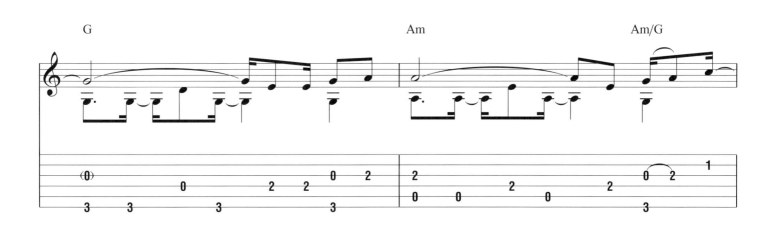

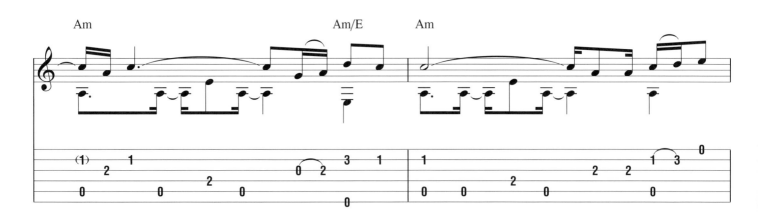

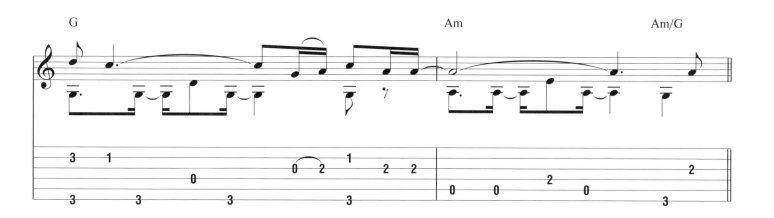

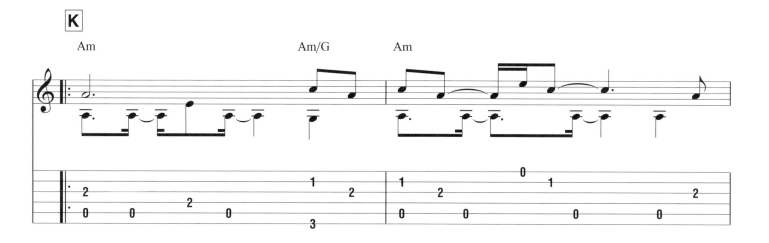

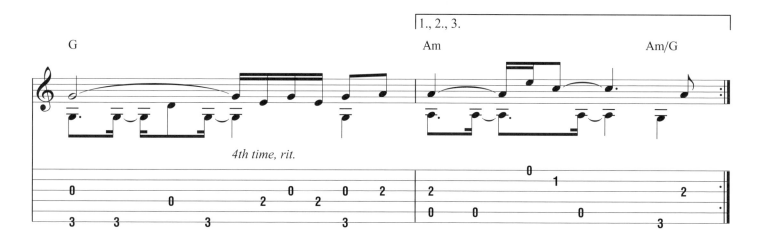

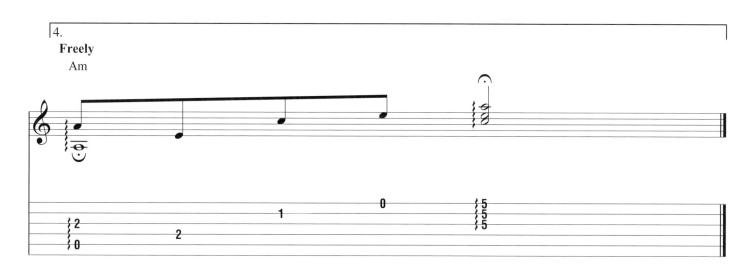

GUITAR NOTATION LEGEND

THE MUSICAL STAFF shows pitches and rhythms and is divided by bar lines into measures. Pitches are named after the first seven letters of the alphabet.

TABLATURE graphically represents the guitar fingerboard. Each horizontal line represents a string, and each number represents a fret.

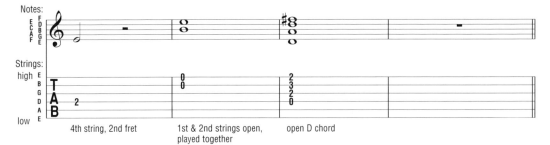

4th string, 2nd fret | 1st & 2nd strings open, played together | open D chord

HALF-STEP BEND: Strike the note and bend up 1/2 step.

WHOLE-STEP BEND: Strike the note and bend up one step.

GRACE NOTE BEND: Strike the note and immediately bend up as indicated.

SLIGHT (MICROTONE) BEND: Strike the note and bend up 1/4 step.

BEND AND RELEASE: Strike the note and bend up as indicated, then release back to the original note. Only the first note is struck.

PRE-BEND: Bend the note as indicated, then strike it.

VIBRATO: The string is vibrated by rapidly bending and releasing the note with the fretting hand.

PALM MUTING: The note is partially muted by the pick hand lightly touching the string(s) just before the bridge.

HAMMER-ON: Strike the first (lower) note with one finger, then sound the higher note (on the same string) with another finger by fretting it without picking.

PULL-OFF: Place both fingers on the notes to be sounded. Strike the first note and without picking, pull the finger off to sound the second (lower) note.

LEGATO SLIDE: Strike the first note and then slide the same fret-hand finger up or down to the second note. The second note is not struck.

SHIFT SLIDE: Same as legato slide, except the second note is struck.

TRILL: Very rapidly alternate between the notes indicated by continuously hammering on and pulling off.

TAPPING: Hammer ("tap") the fret indicated with the pick-hand index or middle finger and pull off to the note fretted by the fret hand.

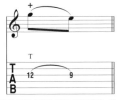

NATURAL HARMONIC: Strike the note while the fret-hand lightly touches the string directly over the fret indicated.

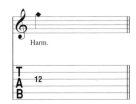

PINCH HARMONIC: The note is fretted normally and a harmonic is produced by adding the edge of the thumb or the tip of the index finger of the pick hand to the normal pick attack.

TREMOLO PICKING: The note is picked as rapidly and continuously as possible.

VIBRATO BAR DIVE AND RETURN: The pitch of the note or chord is dropped a specified number of steps (in rhythm), then returned to the original pitch.

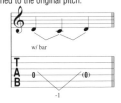

VIBRATO BAR SCOOP: Depress the bar just before striking the note, then quickly release the bar.

VIBRATO BAR DIP: Strike the note and then immediately drop a specified number of steps, then release back to the original pitch.

Additional Musical Definitions

(accent) · Accentuate note (play it louder).

(staccato) · Play the note short.

D.S. al Coda · Go back to the sign (%), then play until the measure marked *"To Coda,"* then skip to the section labelled "**Coda**."

D.C. al Fine · Go back to the beginning of the song and play until the measure marked *"Fine"* (end).

Fill · Label used to identify a brief melodic figure which is to be inserted into the arrangement.

N.C. · Harmony is implied.

 · Repeat measures between signs.

 · When a repeated section has different endings, play the first ending only the first time and the second ending only the second time.